THE BLOOMSBURY TRAIL IN SUSSEX

Virginia Stephen as a child with her mother Adeline

THE BLOOMSBURY TRAIL IN SUSSEX

JUDY MOORE

S.B. Publications

For Christopher and Euly

First published in 1995 by S.B. Publications
Tel: 01323 893498
Email: sbpublications@tiscali.co.uk
Reprinted 1995, 1996, 1997, 1998, 1999, 2001, 2003, 2005

ISBN 1 85770 077 5

Printed by Ethos Productions Ltd.

CONTENTS

Front Cover: Firle Beacon (Jim Redman)

Back cover: Prince Charles in Duncan Grant's Studio, Charleston Farmhouse, March, 1994. The bust of
Virginia Woolf can be seen to the right of Prince Charles; the original bust can be seen in the
garden at Monks House, Rodmell. Angelica Garnett is on the right (Brighton Evening Argus)

Title page: Charleston Farmhouse

ACKNOWLEDGEMENTS

Generous help has been given me by Jim Bartholomew,
Jim Redman and especially by Brigid Chapman without whom
this book would never have been tackled — or completed

INTRODUCTION

B ARELY a month passes, or so it seems, without the publication of a new book about the Bloomsbury Group. There are biographies and autobiographies, rarified recollections, memoirs and essays. There are books about the impact of childhood sexual abuse on Virginia Woolf, books about the importance of frames in her writing, collections of her letters and edited diaries . . . Then there are books by and about people on the Bloomsbury fringe, re-issues of books by Bloomsberries — even a Bloomsbury needlepoint book. Laid end to end they would stretch twice round Gordon Square, London WC1.

The heyday of Bloomsbury was the period between the two world wars, for it was then that public taste finally caught up with the movement's artists and writers. But public taste is fickle, and Bloomsbury fell out of favour in the 1940s until, twenty years later, it was rediscovered by the young. The children of the Sixties — Woodstock, psychedelia, 'love is all you need' — found the Bloomsberries had not only been there but had done it all before them.

Today, Bloomsbury still exerts a powerful fascination, whether for the body of work produced by its members, or for their extraordinary, sexually and emotionally interlinked lives. Quentin Bell's biography of his aunt, Virginia Woolf, the release of the Woolf archive, Michael Holroyd's biography of Lytton Strachey and Hilary Spurling's biography of Vanessa Bell are the foundation stones of the ongoing obsession.

However, this is more of a Sussex book than 'another blooming Bloomsbury book'. It is about the houses which became their Sussex homes — where they lived and loved, wrote their books, painted their pictures and expressed their feelings with an intellectual intensity that set them apart from 'the rural rest.'

These houses — in order of acquisition and/or occupation, which was sometimes consecutive as the various menages moved about — are Little Talland House at Firle, Asham House, Eleanor House and a boat shed at West Wittering, The Grange at Bosham, The Round House in Lewes, Charleston Farmhouse, Monks House, Rodmell and Tilton. In the Church of St Michael and All Angels at Berwick are murals by Duncan Grant, Vanessa Bell and her son Quentin.

Firle Beacon and Tilton

FAMILY BACKGROUND

THE Bloomsbury Group was a coterie of post-Victorian intellectuals, writers and artists who came together in the London home of the Stephens — Vanessa, Thoby, Virginia and Adrian. The quartet set up house in Gordon Square, Bloomsbury when they were orphaned in young adulthood. Their mother, Adeline, had died of rheumatic fever in 1895 and their father, Sir Leslie Stephen, of stomach cancer in 1904.

The young Stephens had a mentally unstable half-sister, Laura, from Leslie's first marriage, and two half-brothers and a half-sister, George, Gerald and Stella Duckworth, from Adeline's first marriage, although none was part of Bloomsbury.

What, then, was Bloomsbury?

Thoby went up to Cambridge where he became a member of the Cambridge Conversazione Society, known as the Apostles. When in London it was the custom of his fellow Apostles — E M Forster, Sydney Waterlow, Desmond MacCarthy, Saxon Sydney Turner, Leonard Woolf, Lytton Strachey, Maynard Keynes, Roger Fry, Gerald Shove, James Strachey and H J Norton — to meet for conversation at 46 Gordon Square where Vanessa and Virginia held a salon.

Molly MacCarthy, Desmond's wife, first coined the term Bloomsberries in 1910 and the phrase Bloomsbury Group came into existence a year or so later. The name of a London borough thus became shorthand for an attitude to life and art. Vita Sackville West called it the Gloomsbury Group.

Other, non-Apostolic members of the Bloomsbury Group were Duncan Grant, introduced by his cousin Lytton Strachey; Francis Birrell; Clive Bell (at Cambridge, but denied membership of the Apostles); Molly MacCarthy; and later Dora Carrington, David Garnett and Marjorie Strachey among others. The younger women members of Bloomsbury — namely Carrington (as she liked to be called), Alix Sargent, Florence and Barbara Hiles — were known as the Bloomsbury Bunnies.

In the Gordon Square house they sat and talked, enjoyed long silences, smoked and drank cocoa and whisky. They were concerned primarily with feeling and the expression of feeling. 'What was felt was right, however it was regarded by society,' explained writer David Gadd. They rejected the social niceties of the upper middle ·class society in which most of them had been reared and enjoyed a freedom of speech and thought that shocked outsiders. In Edwardian England men addressed each other by their surnames and women were always accorded the title Miss or Mrs. The Bloomsberries were the first to sweep away these formalities, calling each other by their given names.

Leonard Woolf, a man who loved accuracy and order, maintained that Bloomsbury did not come fully into existence until 1912, and that the founding members were Virginia and Vanessa, Adrian, Lytton, Clive, Maynard, Duncan, E M Forster, Saxon, Roger, Desmond and Molly and himself. Almost certainly the group had been founded earlier, but Leonard was out of the country at the time, working as a civil servant in Ceylon.

Thoby Stephen died of typhoid fever in 1906, after a holiday in Greece. Shortly afterwards Vanessa agreed to marry Clive Bell, giving the Bloomsberries a second London salon in which to meet and talk.

Members of the group looked after each other when it came to publicising their individual literary and artistic endeavours. They would review each others' books, praise each others' pictures, expound at length about each others' intellectual integrity and the rightness of their attitudes to life and art. The outside world took a rather more varied view with adulation and denigration following each other in waves from the earliest days. Currently a tide of denigration is flowing, yet simultaneously there is a powerful undercurrent of fascination for the cast of players — witness the groaning bookshop shelves and the increasing popularity of such Bloomsbury venues as Charleston, Monks House and Berwick church.

In an essay published in the Daily Mail on August 6, 1994, historian Andrew Robert, pondering on how life in Britain would have been had World War Two never happened, wrote:

'Society's shift into permissiveness probably began with the end of the Great War and the birth of a cultural movement centred on the Bloomsbury Group, sniggering left-wing thinkers who encouraged free love and uncaringly led thousands of people into lives of unhappiness and degradation. The work of E M Forster, Virginia Woolf and Vanessa Bell helped to infect society with cynicism, short-termism, amorality and lack of patriotism.'

Maynard Keynes' biographer, Robert Skidelsky, wrote of Bloomsbury that 'blasphemy was a credo going back to Cambridge days; bawdiness was almost de rigueur'. He also declared that the Bloomsbury painters — Duncan Grant, Vanessa Ball and Roger Fry — were not in the front rank, nor were the Bloomsbury writers, with the exception of Virginia Woolf, although he considered them all first class publicists.

Reviewing Carrington: a life of Dora Carrington, by Gretchen Gerzina, in 1989, (published by John Murray) William Startle wrote:

'Bloody Bloomsbury marches on. As it becomes ever plainer that nothing good —

except perhaps Gerald Brennan — ever emerged from it, its grotty doings are the more devotedly chronicled, from Duncan Grant's porny scrawls to the menage-muddles of the obscurest bisexual neurotic. The fact that the art and ideas produced by the Bloomsberries were inconsiderable only encourages biographers to make free with their lives.'

The Sunday Times's John Carey on Bloomsbury:

'Mostly the reader is torn between trying to remember who is currently going to bed with whom, and wondering if it really matters'.

Writer and actor Dirk Bogarde wrote of 'tiresome Bloomsberries' and added: 'Consider for a moment: the Woolfs, poky-nosed, intellectual, barren sexually, patronising, successful with their little Hogarth Press, and influential. Then poor, silly Ottoline Morrell, scorned, vilified, used as a cheap (but expensive for the Morrells) haven for safe discussion, wine, food and argument far from the horrors and odours of the war.'

A reference to Bloomsbury's conscientious objectors becoming honorary gardeners at Garsington, Bloomsbury groupie Ottoline's country house, in the early years of the 1914–18 War.

Bogarde goes on:

'There were the rather dreary Garnetts; the Bells painting away like anything every lampshade and mantelshelf in primary colours and simplified forms; the awful Gerald Brennan, selfish and whining; the hysterical Gertler who really needed a swift kick up the backside and the rugger-bugger Partridge'.

Bloomsbury was a mutual admiration society, cut off from outside events be they fashion, taste, war or politics. There is a story, possibly apocryphal, of Vanessa asking the man seated next to her at a dinner party if he were interested in politics. The man was Herbert Henry Asquith, the Prime Minister.

Politician and writer Roy Hattersley is of the opinion that the Bloomsberries' emotions were so confused that those who did not have nervous breakdowns themselves brought them about in others. 'The little egocentric group contained at least three figures of authentic genius. John Maynard Keynes changed economics from a gloomy to a hopeful science. Lytton Strachey revolutionised the art of biography. And Virginia Woolf became one of the half dozen truly great English novelists of the twentieth century . . . More conventional authors complained of her contempt for plot, character and dialogue. But although her work lacked form it did not lack discipline. She had invented a new technique, the direct expression of feeling.'

Virginia, the first 'stream of consciousness' writer, also lacked the ability to spell correctly and had only the barest grasp of the rules of punctuation, neither of which detracted from the perfect harmony of her lyrical prose.

Virginia Stephen c.1910

(The Tate Gallery Archive, Vanessa Bell photographic collection, neg 323)

BLOOMSBERRIES IN LOVE

THE Bloomsberries were endlessly fascinated with each other's sexuality. Vanessa was uninhibited, warm, sensual, witty, calm and composed. Virginia, a virgin until she married at the latish age of thirty, was uninhibited only in her thoughts and conversation. She has been described as remote and excitable, humorous and serene, malicious and clever — with 'a deep red velvet voice'. Clive Bell was the archetypal womaniser. Lytton Strachey was a homosexual whose first serious affair was with his cousin, Duncan Grant, and both Lytton and Duncan had affairs with Maynard Keynes. In his nineties, Duncan revealed that Maynard had picked him up in a pub near Victoria Station and invited him back to his rooms in Victoria Street for a bath.

A later lover of Duncan's, David (Bunny) Garnett, became his son-in-law. While Duncan was having an affair with Bunny, who was primarily heterosexual, Vanessa, his painting partner and married to Clive, was having an affair with Roger Fry. This ceased when she fell in love with Duncan, six years her junior, and eventually persuaded him into her bed.

The result was a daughter, Angelica. Bunny was at Charleston Farmhouse when the baby was born and he declared, on seeing her, that one day he would marry her — which he did. Angelica was seventeen before she discovered that Duncan was her father and even older when she learned that her husband had been her father's lover.

There was sexual ambiguity among the female Bloomsberries, too, most notably with Virginia, who had an affair with writer Vita Sackville West who was married to the bi-sexual diplomat and man of letters, Harold Nicolson.

Dora Carrington, an early feminist, chose to look and dress like a man. She fell in love with Lytton Strachey who, although he preferred boys, set up house with her. Then Ralph Partridge fell in love with Carrington, and was himself desired by Lytton who persuaded Dora to marry the young man. Ralph moved into Lytton's house to form a menage a trois which came to a tragic end when Lytton died and Dora killed herself.

Lytton, myopic, squeaky-voiced, witty, clever and snobbish would, declared literary reviewer Christopher Hudson, have had the Kenneth Williams role had there been a Carry on Bloomsbury.

Skidelsky suggested it was the advent of war in 1914 that enabled Bloomsbury to catch up with heterosexuality — there being a shortage of men. Lytton, briefly, became interested in Carrington, Duncan in Vanessa and Maynard in Barbara Hiles (who married Nicholas Bagenal). Later in the war Maynard took Mary Hutchinson, a Strachey cousin, as his mistress. Subsequently she became the long-term mistress of Clive.

After university Leonard Woolf joined the Civil Service and left for Ceylon. Lytton, who had placed himself in a quandary by proposing marriage to Virginia, wrote to Leonard suggesting that he, Leonard, should marry Virginia instead. It was an idea that appealed to Leonard, who had been seeking a way of returning to the Bloomsbury fold after six intellectually arid years in the colonies.

With Leonard back in London, Vanessa and Lytton persuaded Virginia to accept his suit. In the early years of the twentieth century the English were casually offensive about Judaism but Leonard accepted anti-Semitic slights and jokes, rarely defending the faith which he had abandoned when he went up to Cambridge.

He was the son of a barrister, grandson of a tailor. He regarded Virginia as a genius and thought her beautiful and distinguished. He was aware that, because of her eccentric style of dress, some people saw her as strange and laughable — even in Lewes High Street passers-by would nudge each other and comment on her peculiar appearance. And it was her genius, Leonard believed, that accounted in some part for the mental instability that overshadowed her life.

Virginia adored her sister's children and after her marriage she wanted desperately to be a mother, but Leonard decreed that it would be better for her mental health if they remained childless. Was he right or desperately wrong? 'I put my life blood into writing and she (Vanessa) had children,' said Virginia.

A FEW MONTHS AT FIRLE

IN 1911, in one of a pair of incongruous, semi-detached, three-storey Edwardian villas, twenty-nine-year-old Virginia Stephen made her first country home in Sussex. She had been on family holidays in the county as a child — first with her parents in rooms at 9 St Aubyns, Hove in the summer of 1899, and in the same rooms at Easter the following year. As an adult she had stayed with friends at Forest Row in the summer of 1905 and spent the month of August with her youngest brother, Adrian, at The Steps, Playden two years later. At the same time their sister, Vanessa, newly married to Clive Bell, was staying a few miles away — at Curfew Cottage in Rye.

Throughout 1910 Virginia suffered recurring bouts of ill health, and after a period at a rest home in Twickenham she went to Cornwall to recuperate in the countryside near St Ives, where — at Talland House — the Stephen family had spent their summers from 1881 to 1894.

She returned to London in October, still frail, and both medical and family advice was that she should find a quiet cottage in the country to escape the Bloomsbury social whirl.

On December 24, Virginia and Adrian took rooms at the Pelham Arms, an old inn on St Anne's Hill in Lewes. During what must have been a rather strange week for them, away from the family during Christmas, they called on the property agents and toured the area, eventually finding not a cottage but a newly built villa in a village a few miles east of Lewes.

Little Talland House, as Virginia named it after the family's Cornish holiday home, was one of a pair of villas ornamented with concrete beams on pebble dash, and with tile hanging in the Tudor style. They still sit uncomfortably in Firle's one main street, sandwiched between an elegant small Georgian house with glazed black mathematical tiles and a row of cottages built for Lord Gage's estate workers.

Virginia took a lease on the six-year-old house and moved in during January, 1911. In the months that followed she often entertained fellow Bloomsberries in what she euphemistically called her 'cottage in the South Downs'. To Leonard Woolf she admitted that Little Talland House was not a cottage but 'a hideous suburban villa', and her nephew, Quentin Bell, agreed with her. In his biography of Virginia he wrote: '. . . it must be allowed that the house which she actually chose to live in did not contribute to the repose of the village street; it was a raw, red, newly-built, gabled villa'.

Talland House today. Virginia Stephen named it Little Talland House when she rented the villa in 1911

(Judy Moore)

Less raw, less red, but still a pimple, if not quite one of Prince Charles's carbuncles, on the fair face of Firle, the house has acquired a modicum of character with age. The village, beneath the rampart of Firle Beacon, is remote in time and place from the late-twentieth century. It hides from the traffic on the A27 at the end of a winding country lane and is still remarkably feudal — only some eleven of its properties, about fifteen per cent, being privately owned. The others belong to Viscount Gage, whose grand Elizabethan country house, Firle Place, dominates the village.

The Gages have lived in Firle for 500 years, and it was an ancestor of the present viscount who introduced the green plum, the greengage, to England.

In 1911 Firle would have looked very little different from the way it does today. Seemingly set in aspic, it is not the prettiest of villages, yet it has an honest period integrity. In the jargon of the local authority's planning department, it is 'a nucleated settlement within an Area of Outstanding Natural Beauty'.

Leonard Woolf was invited to Virginia's villa for a weekend in September, 1911. Of the visit he wrote: 'It was still the unending summer of that marvellous year, and it seemed as if the clouds would never again darken the sky as we sat reading in Firle Park or walked over the downs. This was the first time that I had seen the South Downs as it were from the inside and felt the beauty of the gentle white curves of the fields between the great green curves of their hollows. I have lived close to them ever since and have learnt that, in all seasons and circumstances, their physical loveliness and serenity can make one's happiness exquisite and assuage one's misery.'

Rupert Brook also spent a weekend with Virginia and on a Sunday morning sat with her in Firle Park writing poetry.

Substantial and comfortable as it was, even without piped water, Little Talland House was by no means the idyllic country retreat Virginia envisaged, and within only a few months she was searching for an alternative. When she found one she sublet the villa to a Bloomsbury associate, Robin Mayor and his wife Beatrice.

Talland House, as it is named today, is privately owned and is not open to the public. However, those on the Bloomsbury trail should visit the village churchyard for it is here that Vanessa Bell and Duncan Grant are buried. Their headstones, simple and stark, stand side by side in a sea of tall, waving grasses.

Asham House as it appeared in 1912

(Drawing by Michael Ward-Sale)

ASHAM HOUSE ELEGANCE

ONE afternoon in October 1911 Virginia Stephen and Leonard Woolf walked up the steep northern escarpment of Firle Beacon and over towards Itford Hill, enjoying one of those calm and mellow days of early autumn when the mist rises from the river valley.

'Do you feel that the days of October melt into each other, the night being almost indistinguishable from the day?' Virginia wrote to Lady Robert Cecil. 'We begin with mist and end with mist. We have about five hours of soft sunshine in the middle.'

Their walk took them down into a hidden valley and there they saw Asham House — elegant, isolated and empty.

To Virginia, tenant of a 'hideous suburban villa', its beautiful proportions, its generous size, its remoteness in a stand of elms and its lovely views across the Ouse Valley to the opposite range of Downs, made it irresistible. Leonard found it 'an extraordinarily romantic looking house'.

Inquiries revealed that the house was to let. It was part of Itford Farm, which had been bought by a Lewes solicitor in 1820. He took on a farm bailiff who lived in the old farmhouse and for himself built Asham House as a summer residence.

It was L-shaped, 'flat, plain, serene, yellow washed' with four bedrooms, large attics and spacious living rooms with French windows opening onto the terrace. It faced west, across the river valley. Beyond the terrace was a lawn bordered by a great meadow, full of sheep, which swept down to the road linking Lewes with the coast.

The name Asham, or Asheham as Virginia liked to spell it, derived from a lost hamlet known as Asseham which, possibly, was the Eshelle of the Domesday Book — an area of some four hides with a population of ten.

The house had been empty for some time. A year before Leonard and Virginia discovered it sculptor Eric Gill, then living in Ditchling, had considered creating a modern Stonehenge on the site but nothing came of the project. The farm, and Asham House, were owned by the solicitor's grand-daughter, who lived in Rugby, and from her Virginia obtained a five year lease on the house.

Leonard proposed to Virginia on January 11, 1912, but her new country house was uppermost in her mind and she did not accept him at once. Two house warming parties which set the pattern for countless gatherings of Bloomsberries at Asham over the next eight years were held at the beginning of February. The first was attended by Leonard, Virginia's brother, Adrian, and Marjorie Strachey, and the second by Vanessa (who, initially, shared the expenses of Asham with her sister), her husband Clive Bell, Adrian, Roger Fry and Duncan Grant.

In the middle of February that year Virginia's pleasure in her new home was interrupted when her always frail mental health — her doctors diagnosed neurasthenia — let her down and she went to Jean Thomas's rest home at Twickenham. She recuperated for much of March and April at Asham House, and by May 29 she was sufficiently recovered to accept Leonard's proposal.

They were married at St Pancras Register Office on August 10, 1912, and had a two-day honeymoon in Sussex, followed by an extended touring holiday that took them first to the Quantocks and then to France, Spain and Italy.

While they were away Vanessa Bell moved into Asham for the winter, arriving at Lewes station with nine pieces of luggage, and a bath. Her current lover, Roger Fry, was with her and her sons, Julian and Quentin, arrived shortly afterwards with their nurse.

With the help of her maid, Sophie Farrell, she set about making the place habitable. They sewed curtains, planted the garden and laid out a badminton court on the lawn. Walter Funnell, the old shepherd who lived in a cottage down the road, was employed to empty the earth closet.

During that first Asham autumn, Vanessa painted, against a background of her new curtains, the picture of brother and sister, Frederick and Jessie Etchells, which is now in the Tate Gallery. Another of her paintings dating from that time is *Landscape with Haystack, Asheham*. She entertained Duncan and Maynard, Molly McCarthy, Saxon Sidney Turner, Oliver Strachey, her brother Adrian and Violet Dickinson — her innate ability to put people at their ease making these visits to Asham peaceful and relaxed.

Virginia and Leonard, back from abroad, made their London home in rooms at 13 Clifford's Inn and thereafter divided their time between London and Sussex, finishing the year with their first Christmas at Asham House.

Living conditions there, even for those days, were extremely primitive, and must have seemed excessively so to the (mainly) well-heeled Bloomsberries. Virginia and Vanessa had been brought up in a large, comfortable London house with servants to see to the cleaning, cooking and the lighting of fires. Leonard's family, too, had been prosperous, as had those of most of their friends and weekend guests.

At Asham the only sanitation was an earth closet in the yard. It was in a tiny building containing a wooden bench, with a hole in the seat. It was Funnell's job to shovel out the night soil from the trap at the back of the building and replace it with fresh. Water had to be pumped from a well into a holding tank each day, and if hot water were needed for a bath, or for washing the dishes, it had to be heated on the stove. There was no electricity, candles and smoky oil lamps providing after dark

Vanessa Bell at Asham

(The Tate Gallery Archive, Vanessa Bell photographic collection, neg R11)

illumination. Wood and coal fires were the only source of heat, and all the cooking was done on a Primus stove.

Leonard encouraged Virginia to cook and, inveterate clock-watcher that he was, he set for her the times she should toil in the kitchen and the times when she should read, write and relax.

Asham House was four miles south of Lewes, four miles north of Newhaven. At weekends Virginia and Leonard travelled by train to Lewes, carrying provisions in knapsacks, and either walked along the river bank or took the fly to Asham. Guests were instructed to order a fly from Slaughter of Friars Walk in Lewes, or take a taxi from Castle Garage in the High Street.

If she ran out of cigarettes when she was there Virginia would walk over the railway line at Southease Halt, across the river by the little bridge and take a short-cut via the water meadows to Rodmell on the far side of the valley, where there was a handy village store.

Despite the privations of Asham it became a dearly-loved home. Virginia sallied forth to pick mushrooms and blackberries on the Downs, she made jams and bottled fruits, and kept dogs, cats, hens and geese. 'It's far the loveliest place in the world,' she wrote to a friend.

In the last year of peace, when twilight fell on the old order in Europe, so a twilight began to fall on Virginia. Her depressions and mental disturbances deepened, and she had delusions and an eating disorder.

In March she and Leonard spent a weekend with the Gills at Ditchling, on the other side of Lewes. There, with Douglas Pepler, Gill had founded the Guild of SS Joseph and Dominic, a group of artists and craftsmen and women inspired by religious ideals. In September, 1913, Virginia attempted suicide with an overdose of Veronal. Her stomach was pumped and she suffered a prolonged mental breakdown. She was taken to recuperate at Dalingridge Place near East Grinstead, the Sussex home of her half-brother George Duckworth.

She and Leonard spent two months at Dalingridge Place, and at one time four mental nurses were in attendance. In November the Woolfs returned to Asham with two of the nurses — whose reaction to the lack of sanitation after the comforts of the Duckworth home can only be guessed at.

For a period from the end of 1913 until the following autumn, when the Woolfs had given up the lease at Clifford's Inn, Asham House became their principal home. Virginia was well enough to go house-hunting in London by the summer, and in October they moved temporarily to 17 The Green, Richmond.

They were on the move again just a few months later when they found Hogarth House, also in Richmond, which proved ideal for the printing and publishing house they planned (The Hogarth Press).

It was said that Asham House was haunted, and often Leonard and Virginia heard strange noises at night, as if people were walking from room to room, opening and shutting doors, sighing and whispering. The ghostly happenings are believed to have inspired Virginia's story, *A Haunted House*, published posthumously in *A Haunted House and Other Stories* (1944).

Of Asham Leonard wrote: 'I have never known a house which had such a strong character, personality of its own — romantic, gentle, melancholy, lovely . . . one often had a feeling as if one were living under water in the depths of the sea behind the thick, rough glass of the room's long windows — a sea of green trees, green grass, green air.'

This was an ambience that the Woolfs re-created later at Monks House where their green-painted drawing room, shaded by a great vine at the windows, had a submarine quality.

Leonard was swimming in Seaford Bay when he heard that Britain was about to go to war. He had cycled to the coast that hot, sunny day — August 1, 1914 — and was cooling off in the sparkling water when a fellow swimmer, a Metropolitan policeman holidaying in Seaford, said that war was about to be declared. He told Leonard he had received a telegram recalling him to London, and there could be only one reason.

At Asham House there was no telephone and no newspapers were delivered. The next day, a Sunday, Leonard walked into Lewes to hear what was afoot. He joined a group of townsfolk outside the post office, traditionally the place where notices were posted and announcements made, and learned that Britain was at war with Germany.

Four of Leonard's brothers joined up immediately and urged him to go with them. He found himself in a quandary. He was against the war but, unlike many of his friends, he was not a conscientious objector and he believed Germany should be resisted. He was also anxious about Virginia and discussed the situation with her doctor who agreed she should not be left alone. The doctor gave him a certificate exempting him from military service 'because of his nervous disabilities and an inherited nervous tremor'. Leonard did not entirely agree with this assessment, but when he was called up he produced the certificate and was sent home.

On the day war broke out Virginia and Leonard crossed the bridge over the Ouse and walked up on to the Downs behind the cliff edge at what is now Peacehaven. Charles Nevill was just then formulating his plans for a garden city by the sea, but on that August day in 1914 there were only a handful of cottages on the clifftop, a farmhouse, tea rooms and vast empty spaces — the Downland turf starred with a myriad wild flowers and bird song carried on the sea breezes.

Leonard blamed the war for what happened on that clifftop — the collapse of Nevill's New Anzac on Sea, as he called it, or Lureland, and the sale of cheap plots on the Manhattan-style grid laid out across miles of empty Downland, on which all manner of shacks were built.

He described the desecration as 'part of the destruction of the civilisation, the way of life, which existed in Sussex before 1914'.

In his autobiography, *Beginning Again*, published in 1964, he said that no man would, then (fifty years later) walk to Peacehaven from Asham, 'for on the way he would see lovely downs spattered with ugly buildings and, when he got there, he would find all round him, as far as the eye could see, miles of disorderly ugliness, shoddiness, and squalor'.

After Vanessa took Charleston Farmhouse near Firle, in 1916, Virginia found country life even more enticing. The sisters visited each other often and frequently met at Firle Post Office with picnic baskets to spend the day in the woods below Firle Beacon.

There were Bloomsbury house parties at Asham throughout the war, and Virginia always warned intending visitors to bring their own meat, sugar and butter, or their ration cards, as provisions were difficult to come by.

A German Zeppelin was spotted over Asham one day and, at other times, when the wind was in the right quarter, the pounding of guns in France was clearly heard in the Ouse Valley.

To help in the house the Woolfs employed Walter Funnell's wife, Edith, and were considerably amused by her Sussex dialect — which has now all but died out. They were completely foxed when Mrs Funnell told them, after a night of violent winds, that her flowers were all 'dishabille' — the dialect contains a great deal of Norman French.

In 1917 the Woolfs had to renew the lease on Asham House, and they were told that after the war the farm was to be divided in two, and Asham would be needed for the second bailiff. They were given a yearly lease for the duration and at the end of the war they received a year's notice.

At first, Virginia thought of making their country home in Cornwall and taking 'a tiny cottage in Firle'. Later she abandoned the idea because of the distance from London, and looked instead for a house close to Lewes. What she found — and bought for £300 in June, 1919 — was The Round House, right in the centre of the county town. A month later the Woolfs discovered that Monks House in the Ouse Valley village of Rodmell was on the market and this became their last, and most permanent Sussex home.

A BOAT SHED — AND BOSHAM

IN Virginia's pre-war days at Asham Vanessa Bell was an almost constant visitor and shared the expenses of the household with her sister. She was an unorthodox and complex woman. When her first child, Julian, was born in 1908 she became obsessed with the baby and her husband, Clive, feeling neglected, had a serious flirtation with his sister-in-law, Virginia. A year later he rekindled his affair with Mrs Raven-Hill, who had seduced him when he was eighteen.

The Bells' second son, Quentin (first named Gratian, then Claudian) was born in August, 1910, and in the same year Vanessa began a three year affair with painter and critic, Roger Fry. Clive, Vanessa and Roger, whose wife Helen was confined to an asylum in 1910, holidayed across Europe together, and were later joined by Duncan Grant who, at the time, was having an affair with his cousin, Lytton Strachey. He was simultaneously in love with Adrian Stephen and was attracted to George Mallory, the mountaineer who died on Everest.

In 1913 Roger, Vanessa and Duncan launched the Omega Workshops, taking commissions for murals, paintings, stained glass windows, painted furniture, mosaics, rugs, fabrics and pottery. Among young artists and craftsmen associated with the studios at 33 Fitzroy Square in Bloomsbury were Frederick Etchells, the sculptor Gaudier-Brzeska and Edward Wadsworth.

Omega, which according to Vanessa's biographer Frances Spalding, was 'anti-taste, anti-refinement, anti-expense', lasted only six years. The venture lost money and public taste changed. In June, 1919, a sale was organised and the entire stock was sold off.

Vanessa and Duncan, who were painting partners for life, were, for a short period, sexual partners as well. When he was in his eighties Duncan confided to his friend, Paul Roche, that he had first had sexual relations with Vanessa at a Sitwell house party — and that Clive had walked through the room and told them not to stop on his account.

Duncan spent the summer of 1914 in an old boat shed at West Wittering in West Sussex. It had been converted by Slade professor Henry Tonks into a studio with bathroom and kitchen and had a wonderful view across the estuary to Hayling Island. Next door was Eleanor House which St John (Jack) and Mary Hutchinson used as a summer residence. Jack was a barrister, Mary a cousin of Lytton, and

Clive's mistress. Duncan was visited in the boat shed by Adrian and Maynard, Lytton and Ka Cox and when David (Bunny) Garnett joined the party they raided Professor Tonks's wine store and, according to Bunny's diary, 'drank it in the sunlight and fought drunkenly and lustfully'.

Vanessa arrived in West Wittering in early summer, having left the children in London with their nurse. At first she stayed at Eleanor House, then moved into the boat shed with Duncan, where they were joined by Bunny for a time in a Bohemian threesome. When Clive and the children turned up she moved with them into The Grange at Bosham — and Duncan came too. Her previous lover, Roger Fry, was a frequent visitor and there was a period of socialising between Clive, his mistress and her husband, his wife and her two lovers.

The First World War brought an end to this unorthodox West Sussex idyll. The introduction of conscription in 1916 for all men aged between eighteen and forty one had an immediate impact on the male members of the Bloomsbury Group.

Clive was not eligible for military service on medical grounds because of a rupture sustained many years before. Duncan and Bunny, both pacifists, registered as conscientious objectors, and were directed to do agricultural work.

In search of such employment they set off for Suffolk where a recently deceased Grant relative had left a six acre fruit and vegetable farm. Duncan's father, Major Bartle Grant, was overseeing the estate and was not best pleased when his son and Bunny — 'your friend Garbage' — arrived to work there. As a military man he had hopes of a distinguished army career for his son but he allowed the pair to move into the farmhouse, Wissett Grange, and try their hand at working on the land. Vanessa joined them there with her two children and two servants.

In May Duncan and Bunny had to appear before Blything Tribunal in Suffolk to seek exemption from military service. Their application was refused, but they appealed and, with Maynard Keynes, then a senior Treasury officer, speaking on their behalf, the court found in their favour. However, they were told that they could not be self-employed at Wissett and were ordered to find farm work elsewhere. It was fortuitous that, at the time the appeal ruling was made known, Virginia wrote from Asham with details of a farmhouse available near Firle. Vanessa at once travelled to Sussex to see it, with the hope that there would be agricultural work for the two men in the area. The farmhouse was called Charleston — a name which was to become synonymous with Bloomsbury.

THE MOVE TO CHARLESTON

FIRST impressions of Charleston Farmhouse were not favourable. Vanessa had a difficult cross country journey from Suffolk, spent the night at Asham, and next morning cycled along the dusty Lewes–Eastbourne road to find the old farmhouse at the end of a long, rough track. It belonged to the Gages and was let to, but not occupied by a tenant farmer, Mr Stacey, who was willing to sublet. A point in its favour was that a farmer called Hecks of New House Farm, Chalvington, had work for both Duncan and Bunny, but Vanessa was still not sure what to do and went home to London without making any commitments.

She was back in Sussex two days later to take another look at the house — and decided to rent it. It was a decision which led to sixty years of occupancy and the founding of a charitable trust that would take Charleston's Bloomsbury connection into the next century.

The move from Suffolk was a massive undertaking. There were dozens of parcels and suitcases, pieces of furniture, rolls of canvases and easels, bicycles, a dog, rabbits, a sack of artichokes and the children to be organised. The railway company charged nineteen shillings excess baggage.

The children stayed in London while Vanessa set about making the old farmhouse habitable. She faced a formidable task. The part seventeenth- part eighteenth-century house, on even earlier foundations, is a rambling structure with many low-ceilinged rooms and it had been empty and neglected for some years. Living conditions were, as they had been at Asham, primitive — although there was at least a WC.

In the Domesday Book the site is called Cerlocestone. In 1916 the extensive grounds included a paddock, an orchard, a large pond and an old tennis court which was knee high in grass.

Vanessa hunted round the second-hand shops in Lewes for furniture and arranged for some pieces to be sent down from her London home.

Maynard Keynes contributed mattresses from Maples. Once the house was ready it was quickly occupied and a daily routine was established. Duncan and Bunny would set off early each morning to walk the three and a half miles to work in Farmer Heck's fields, and Vanessa would settle down to paint in one of the bedrooms she had converted to a studio.

Vanessa Bell with her sons Quentin and Julian at Charleston
(The Tate Gallery Archive, Vanessa Bell photographic collection, neg Q44)

Over the following three years she and Duncan decorated and ornamented the house, painting the walls, the mantelpieces, doors, walls and furniture. The grey that Vanessa used often as a background colour was her own creation and was to become her signature colour . It provided a warm base for the decorations and is still in use on noticeboards in Charleston to this day.

From 1916 to 1919 the farmhouse, furnished, according to Quentin, for comfort rather than style and decorated by artists more concerned with beauty than with taste, was the permanent home of Vanessa, Duncan and Bunny.

Despite the harsh conditions and minimal sanitation there was no shortage of guests. They would arrive on the Eastbourne train from London, alight at Glynde and walk over the fields; or go on to Berwick in the hope of finding a taxi at the station there.

The house was cold and there was no hot water. When Duncan and Bunny came home, tired and hungry from the work in the fields, wartime shortages often meant that they did not have enough to eat. Vanessa kept ducks, chickens and rabbits to supplement their diet but they all suffered, Duncan in particular. He became so ill during the severe weather of January 1918 that Vanessa obtained a medical certificate which excused him from afternoon work for two months.

Life at Charleston in those wartime years was hard, even though there were servants to cope with the cooking, cleaning and the laundry. Every drop of water had to be pumped from the well and this made having a bath a major undertaking as buckets full of water had to be heated on the stove and carried to the tub.

It was, however, a happy place. When Clive was there he would take the children for walks, go out with his dog and gun to stock the larder, or retire to his room with his pipe and tobacco pouch to write. There were rock cakes and home made scones for tea and a good dinner in the evening, after which everyone retired to the garden room. Classical music was played on the wind up gramophone, cheroots were lit, brandy handed round and Vanessa took out her knitting or embroidery.

The unconventional triangular relationship between the three occupants worked well on the surface, although there were fights and jealousies when Duncan discovered that Bunny had women in London. Vanessa nursed a passionate — and for her far too infrequently fulfilled — love for Duncan. On a spring day in 1918 when Bunny was away Duncan noted in his diary, not romantically, or affectionately but factually, that he 'copulated with her'. Virginia, always to be relied upon for the exact phrase, described their situation as 'a left-handed marriage.'

Unorthodox as she was in her attitude to marriage, Vanessa was a devoted mother to her children. She decided to set up a school at Charleston for her own offspring and other children and engaged Eva Edwards as a governess. However such a Bohemian household was not what this young woman had been accustomed to and she left after only six weeks.

Roger Fry then sent along a Mrs Brereton, who had nursed his wife Helen. She was the estranged wife of a clergyman and had two children, one of whom, Anne, she brought with her to Charleston. They were joined by a young man, Henry Moss, who was to be a tutor at the school.

An advertisement for pupils, quoting fees of £100 a year, was put in *Nation* but although there were places for eight children, only two day boys and one boarder, Mrs Brereton's nephew, joined Julian, Quentin and Anne. Not surprisingly the school lasted for only a term in 1918. When, a year later, Vanessa discovered Mrs Brereton was writing a novel based on the Charleston household, she was immediately asked to leave.

It was particularly hard to find domestic help in the war years when there was more exciting and lucrative work for young women in the munitions factories. A Scottish girl, Emily, was taken on as parlourmaid and later her sister Jenny joined her as cook. Neither proved satisfactory, being unreliable and lazy.

But staff problems were forgotten when, at the age of thirty eight Vanessa found she was expecting Duncan's child — the outcome of that night of passion in the spring. Her husband, Clive, did the decent thing and agreed to be named as the father.

Vanessa had a difficult pregnancy. She almost lost the baby after a bad fall, and had to rest for the remainder of her term. Duncan, in the belief that an embryo could hear, insisted that she listened to music during this period of enforced idleness.

In the eighth month of her pregnancy the Armistice brought the war to an end and Duncan and Bunny, freed from their farm work, talked about becoming picture dealers. Duncan agreed to stay on at Charleston until the baby was born, after which he planned to return to London.

It was at 2am on Christmas morning that Vanessa, who was hoping for another boy, one who would inherit his natural father's genius, was safely delivered of a girl.

Bunny, still at Charleston, wrote to Lytton Strachey: 'I think of marrying it: when she is twenty I shall be 46 — will it be scandalous?'

A nurse was employed to care for Vanessa and the baby but she left the same day, appalled by the state of the house under the slovenly Scots girls. Emily was sacked and Virginia's maid, Nellie Boxall, arrived on loan to take charge of the household. Vanessa named the baby Susannah Paula, changed her mind and called her Claudia, then registered her as Helen Vanessa and finally named her Angelica.

In 1919 the family moved back to London, keeping Charleston on for weekends and holidays. They found that war had changed Bloomsbury, a term that was being used by press and public to label those who were never part of the group, such as T S Eliot, the Sitwells and Aldous Huxley.

The real Bloomsberries fought back and set up the Memoir Club, members being the original Bloomsberries plus, from time to time, strictly vetted newcomers. They met in each other's homes and read autobiographical essays.

'Like the Pre-Raphaelites, Bloomsbury really began to exist in the public imagination at the moment when the original group had dispersed,' wrote Vanessa's biographer, Frances Spurling.

The post office and village store at Firle — little changed from the years of World War One when Vanessa at Charleston and Virginia at Asham would rendezvous there for picnics in the woods below Firle Beacon

(Judy Moore)

THE ROUND HOUSE

IT was after a row with her sister at Charleston that Virginia Woolf, under threat of eviction from Asham House, saw, fell in love with and bought The Round House in Lewes, in1919. On impulse she paid £300 for the property to the estate agent Arthur Wycherley, and returned to London the same day. Leonard was away and knew nothing of the transaction. Later she wrote to Vanessa claiming that it was her sister's 'severity' that had plunged her into 'the recklessness of the purchase'.

'We've bought a house in Lewes — on the spur of the moment,' she wrote to Dora Carrington. 'It's the butt end of an old windmill, so that all the rooms are either completely round or semi-circular.' She was a little anxious about what Leonard would say. 'I've rather forgotten what it is like,' she confided to Vanessa.

The Round House is in Pipe Passage, a narrow twitten that follows the line of the old town wall. In mediaeval times it was a sentry walk within the parapet. From the twitten there is a dramatic view of the keep of Lewes Castle, made even more spectacular after dark when the ruins are floodlit.

The passage is named after the clay pipe-making business that operated there early in the nineteenth century. The remains of a kiln can be seen on a tiny patch of waste ground where a fig tree flourishes. The site was excavated in 1956 and hundreds of broken clay pipes were found.

The Round House is the base of a corn mill built in 1800 at a cost of £600, raised by public subscription. It was to have been built on the summit of Brack Mount, Lewes Castle's second motte, but permission was refused and another site, high up on the town wall to catch the wind, was chosen.

It seems the mill was not well patronised and within a few years it was sold to William Smart, who used it to grind corn until 1819 when the upper works were taken down and the base converted into a house — exactly 100 years before Virginia Woolf was so captivated by the little round cottage.

Leonard was magnanimous about her purchase. Some weeks later he went with her to inspect the place and they both realised it was a mistake. What they really wanted was a house in the country, not a small cottage in the middle of Lewes.

But it is an ill wind . . . Had Virginia not bought The Round House, the Woolfs would not have been in Lewes on that day and would not have seen the poster announcing the sale by auction of Monks House in Rodmell, a cottage that they

The Round House, Lewes — once the base of a windmill — that Virginia Woolf bought on impulse in 1919

(Toby Canham)

already knew, and one that was much more suited to their needs. On their instructions, Wycherley put The Round House back on the market and prepared to bid on their behalf for Monks House. The sale took place in the White Hart Hotel on July 1 and the Woolfs set their limit at £800. The bidding quickly reached £600, to Virginia's consternation, after which they were in competition with only one other bidder. The hammer fell at £700, and Monks House was theirs.

Tenuous links between Bloomsbury and revolutionary and free thinker Thomas Paine were forged by Virginia's impulse purchase of The Round House. Almost directly opposite the point where Pipe Passage meets Lewes High Street is Bull House where Tom Paine, an excise man, lodged with tobacconist Samuel Ollive when he took up his duties in Lewes in 1768. Later he married Ollive's daughter, Elizabeth, and took over the snuff and tobacco business when his father-in-law died.

Lewesians like to boast that the germ of the idea that led to Britain losing her American colonies was sown in Tom Paine's mind, on the ancient bowling green within the castle precincts. The game played then, and now, was that enjoyed by Francis Drake on Plymouth Ho as he awaited the Spanish Armada. It is played on an irregular patch of quite roughish grass — no velvet greensward here — with woods heavily biassed to overcome the undulations.

Paine had been playing one day with friends, and discussing world affairs, when his companion, a Mr Verrall, observed that 'the King of Prussia was the best fellow in the world for a king, he had so much of the devil in him'.

In his biography of Paine, WT Sherwin wrote, in 1810: 'This trifling observation led Paine to reflect that if it were necessary for a king to have so much of a devil in him, kings might very well be dispended with. This, quite unintentionally, gave him the idea of writing *The Rights of Man*.'

Paine's bowling partner was almost certainly William Verrall, landlord of the

THE ESTATE OF JACOB VERRALL, DECEASED.

RODMELL & PIDDINGHOE,
SUSSEX
On the road from Lewes to Newhaven

Particulars and Conditions of Sale
OF THE VALUABLE

Freehold & Copyhold Properties

"MONKS HOUSE," an old-fashioned Residence and three-quarters of an acre of Garden (with possession).

"THE FORGE HOUSE " with Blacksmith's Shop, Garden, and Stabling.

A PLOT OF BUILDING LAND with Corrugated Iron Building thereon.

A DETACHED DWELLING HOUSE at the Crossways with Garden and Corner Building Site, all situate in Rodmell Parish.

A DETACHED DWELLING HOUSE known as The Post Office, and THREE COTTAGES at Harping Hill in Piddinghoe Parish.

which will be offered for Sale by Auction, by

MESSRS.

ST. JOHN SMITH & SON

AT

THE WHITE HART HOTEL, LEWES.

On Tuesday, 1st July, 1919

at HALF PAST THREE o'clock in the afternoon, by Order of the Executors of the late Mr. Jacob Verrall.

The properties may be viewed by arrangement with the respective tenants and Particulars and Conditions of Sale may be obtained at The White Hart Hotel, Lewes ; of Henry J. Hillman, Esq., Solicitor, Lewes ; or of Messrs. St. John Smith & Son, Land Agents and Surveyors, 18, Station Street, Lewes ; 2, Gloucester Place, Seaford (Tel. No. 187) ; and High Street, Uckfield (Tel. No. 18).

From the sale catalogue for Monks House

White Hart Hotel. The Woolfs bought Monks House after the timely, for them, death of one of William's descendants, Jacob Verrall.

In 1774 Tom Paine left Lewes — and his wife — and set sail for America where he became a signatory of the Declaration of Independence.

Another connection between the Woolfs and the revolutionary is the White Hart itself. It was there in the eighteenth century that Paine established the Headstrong Club, whose members gathered weekly to discuss weighty affairs of the moment. They met in the panelled first floor room above the hotel entrance — the same room in which the auction of Monks House took place.

The Headstrong Club was re-established a few years ago after a lapse of some two centuries, and its members commissioned Julian Bell, Vanessa Bell's grandson, Virginia Woolf's great-nephew, to paint a memorial portrait of Tom Paine for a niche in the town's Market Tower.

Julian's painting, see page 88, replaced a strange collage, unveiled with great ceremony in 1993, that attracted such public hostility that it was removed shortly afterwards to the town hall.

The Round House is in private ownership and is not open to the public.

CHARLESTON: THE TWENTIES

IN London Vanessa managed to find someone to look after her new baby. The nursemaid she engaged was sixteen-year-old Grace Germany who became a valued member of the household and stayed on long after Angelica grew up. She married Walter Higgens from Firle and they had a son, John, who was born at Charleston. A large picture of Grace working in the kitchen, painted by Vanessa, who called her 'the angel of Charleston', still hangs in the farmhouse.

In the immediate postwar period there were changes in the emotional relationships of the Charleston Bloomsberries. Bunny became a bookseller in London and embarked on a love affair with the Duchess of Marlborough's lady gardener. His place in Duncan's affections was taken by a string of young men — the brothers Angus and Douglas Davidson, the sculptor Stephen Tomlin, Austrian Franzi von Haas, artist Peter Morris, painter Robert Medley and dancer Rupert Doone. Duncan was always looking for romance and had countless liaisons, even into his old age, each threatening scandal and even imprisonment since homosexual acts between men were illegal until 1967.

He and Vanessa lived intimate but separate lives, married in all but name and bed. Vanessa knew that to keep him by her side she had to give him free reign, and accept his lovers.

The relative tranquillity of their lives in Sussex was shattered in 1921 when Mr Stacey said he wanted Charleston back. But after a great deal of negotiation Vanessa managed to obtain a fourteen-year renewal of the lease. In the event the tenancy lasted sixty years — until Duncan's death in 1978.

Clive Bell, Julian, Quentin and Maynard Keynes
(The Tate Gallery Archive, Vanessa Bell photographic collection, neg U16)

35

Duncan Grant with his daughter Angelica at Charleston
(The Tate Gallery Archive, Vanessa Bell photographic collection, neg H34)

Once the question of tenure had been settled satisfactorily a series of home improvements was started at Charleston. A builder from Uckfield, a Mr Durrant, was given a £250 contract to build a vaulted studio to a design by Roger Fry. At the same time an old dairy next to the studio was converted into a ground floor bedroom for Vanessa. It had a bath and French doors to the garden.

The extension enclosed a small plot that had been a chicken run. A little pond was dug here and a fig tree planted — the children called it 'Grant's Folly'.

Vanessa's black and red painted upstairs bedroom was turned into a library and a small attic room was converted to a second studio. In the dining room a bricked up inglenook fireplace was uncovered and a new heating system was installed but, even modernised, Charleston never rivalled Tilton, the farmhouse just up the track that Maynard Keynes acquired in 1925.

Clive wrote to Virginia: 'Charleston is frankly disappointing, and less commodious than a Sabine farm. But Nessa doesn't care a rap — not she.' His father died in 1927 and he used some of his substantial inheritance to refurbish the farmhouse but it was not until 1933 that Charleston was connected to the main electricity supply.

In spite of the inconveniences at the farmhouse family holidays there were always fun. The boys, Julian and Quentin, produced a daily news sheet, the *Charleston Bulletin*, in which they ran stories and comments on the activities of the household and the guests. In the summer they staged open air productions of plays and tableaux vivants — among them a performance in French of Moliere's *Les Precieuses Ridicules*. Making her theatrical debut in these shows was their little sister, actress-to-be Angelica, who had grown into a sturdy child with a mind of her own. Another regular member of the cast was Janie Bussy, Duncan's cousin.

In 1925 Vanessa again set about establishing a summer school. Marjorie Strachey was put in charge of it and the pupils were the Bell children; Anastasia and Igor Anrep, children of Roger's new love Helen Anrep; Christopher and Nicholas Henderson (the latter was to become British Ambassador to the United States) and Barbara Bagenal's daughter Judith. It lasted for two years — a little longer than the earlier school which folded after a term.

In 1927 the Bells bought a car — as had the Woolfs at Rodmell — and together the extended family explored Sussex. Vanessa would set off as evening fell to paint the new harbour works at Newhaven, or the banks of the Cuckmere at sunset. There were picnics at High and Over and excursions to Bodiam Castle, Herstmonceux Castle and Micheham Priory. Old photographs show that even in high summer the picnickers dressed as if off to the Arctic in thick socks and woollen jumpers, felt hats and, in Virginia's case, a fur coat.

Vanessa was a keen amateur photographer, an interest inherited from her great aunt, photographic pioneer Julia Margaret Cameron. In the early years she did her own developing and printing but she ran into trouble when she took a roll of film into a chemist's shop in Lewes to be developed. She was brusquely told, when she went to collect it, that the young ladies who worked there were upset by her shots of naked bodies.

In 1927 Charleston gained a rival in the family's affections, although they continued to spend August and September at the farmhouse.

Vanessa discovered the magic of the Midi when she rushed to Duncan's bedside after he fell ill while visiting his mother and his aunt, Daisy McNeil. They were at Roland Penrose's Villa des Mimosas in Cassis, near Marseilles, which so enchanted Vanessa that she at once began looking for a second holiday home for the family in the area. She found a ruined cottage, called La Bergere, in the middle of a field at Cassis, and took a ten-year lease on it.

TILTON

THE farmhouse John Maynard Keynes made his country home is a few hundred yards from Charleston, with which it is shares a boundary. It is off the long rough track from Swingates on the A27, and is close to Tilton Wood, an ancient semi-natural woodland.

In 1925, when Maynard negotiated with Lord Gage's Firle estate for the lease, the two storey house was in a dilapidated state. But it was spacious and had great potential. He was delighted to discover that in the eleventh century it had been owned by a de Cahagnes, the original name of the Keynes family.

Maynard, an old Etonian, an undergraduate and Fellow of Kings College, Cambridge, an economist and a mandarin at the Treasury, could trace his family back to 1066 when William de Cahagnes, a vassal of Robert de Mortain, William the Conqueror's half brother, was given land in what were to become the English counties of Northamptonshire, Sussex (Horsted Keynes), Buckinghamshire and Cambridgeshire.

From the day the Bells moved into Charleston Maynard had been a regular visitor — so regular, in fact, that he helped pay the rent. He loved Charleston, in an upstairs room of which he wrote *The Economic Consequences of Peace*, and he spent a lot of time working in the garden, weeding the paths with his penknife.

When he fell in love with Lydia Lopokova, a dancer with Diaghilev's Ballet Russe, and proposed to her, he started looking for a country home close to the Bloomsberries in Sussex. Tilton seemed the obvious choice. From just across the fields he could continue his long, close friendship with Vanessa, Duncan and Clive, and be only minutes away from the Woolfs at Rodmell.

But the happy country life he envisioned with his friends was not to be. Vanessa, Virginia and Leonard, Duncan and Clive had no time for Lydia. She was a frivolous, high spirited woman, and his friends warned him not to marry her. They did not want Lydia in their charmed Bloomsbury circle, fearing she would dilute the elite group.

Virginia thought her pathetic — a person whose only contribution to a conversation was 'a shriek, two dances then silence'. 'We prefer reason to any amount of high spirits, Lydia's pranks put us all on edge', she wrote in a letter to Jacques Raverat.

Yet Lydia's inconsequential chatter, her eccentric use of English, her high spirits, enchanted Maynard who was quick to defend her against the highbrow Bloomsberries.

Lydia, as much an artist in her own field as Maynard's friends were in theirs, knew what they thought of her and longed to be clever and intellectual. Maynard wanted his Bloomsbury friends to accept her and he asked Vanessa if Lydia could stay at Charleston for the summer in 1924.

Vanessa was horrified, and told him he would have to choose between his friends and Lydia. However, she had second thoughts about this ungrateful response towards the man who had provided long term financial support to the occupants of Charleston and allowed the couple to stay for a week over Easter.

This visit did nothing to change the Bloomsberries' attitude to Lydia. Vanessa even considered giving up Charleston and moving to Norfolk or Yorkshire when she heard that Maynard had leased Tilton and she would have his wife as a neighbour.

Skidelsky summed up the situation concisely: 'Keynes was the rich, generous, worldly, slightly wicked uncle to the Charleston family, which is why his marriage to someone completely outside it came as a shock to them,' he wrote in his biography of the great economist. It came as even more of a shock to Duncan, who had been, until then, Maynard's heir.

Lydia and Maynard were married on August 4, 1925, at St Pancras register office, where Virginia and Leonard had been married, also in August, thirteen years previously. They moved temporarily into a house in Iford, near Rodmell, as Tilton was still at that time tenanted, and made Gordon Square in Bloomsbury their London home. In the autumn they went on a belated honeymoon to Russia where Maynard was introduced to Lydia's family. He combined the honeymoon with work, representing Cambridge at the bicentennial celebration of the Russian Academy of Sciences.

When they moved into Tilton in March, 1926, Maynard began an ambitious programme of extension and modernisation. Over the next few years he created a library, built a new wing, installed electricity and the telephone, and had a boiler fitted in the cellar to pipe hot air through grilles to supplement the coal fires.

His architect friend, George Kennedy, uncle of young Richard Kennedy who wrote humorously of working for Virginia and Leonard at The Hogarth Press, supervised the alterations.

In spite of a marked coolness from Charleston, the couple enjoyed being married, loved the countryside and were happy in their Sussex home. Lydia sunbathed naked in the courtyard and Maynard acquired an interest in agriculture, taking over, in the 1930s, the whole of Tilton farm from the Firle estate. He kept pigs, cattle and sheep, grew fruit and vegetables in sufficient abundance to send some to market, and arranged shooting parties.

Although very much the country squire when at Tilton, Maynard never abandoned his Treasury persona and often wore his city suit, homburg and black overcoat when inspecting the crops and stock on his rural acres.

A staff of five looked after their needs, including Ruby Coles, the housekeeper, chauffeur/gardener Edgar Wallace from Firle who married Ruby, and his aunt who became Lydia's personal maid.

Maynard was a serious collector of works of art. On the walls at Tilton were paintings by Picasso and Braque, Cezanne, Renoir, Degas, Seurat and Sickert. In the library was an extensive collection of Elizabethan and Stuart literature.

The paintings were hung high up to be out of reach of burglars, so at eye level the walls appeared strangely blank. They were also individually wired up so that if tampered with the alarm would ring in Lewes Police Station. According to Quentin his mother and the rest of the Charleston set believed that they had only to look at the pictures to have a posse of police racing along the A27.

After his death Maynard's collection went first to Kings College, Cambridge, then on permanent loan to the Fitzwilliam Museum.

He was remarkably casual about one of his first acquisitions — a Cezanne still life which he bought at auction in Paris in 1918. Austen Chamberlain, with whom he had been attending post-war talks, gave him a lift in his car from Newhaven to Swingates corner where Maynard alighted with several pieces of luggage and the Cezanne. Unable to carry it all he hid the painting in the hedge, picked up his suitcases and trudged up the long track to Charleston. When Duncan and Bunny heard what he had left behind they may well have broken the four minute mile — years before Bannister — in their dash to retrieve the painting.

Many of Lydia's friends from the world of ballet were among the visitors to Tilton during the inter-war years. The guest list included such greats as Robert Helpmann, Frederick Ashton, Balanchine and Anton Dolin and the theatre was represented by Vivien Leigh.

Maynard and Lydia maintained casual contact with the Woolfs who, traditionally, spent part of Christmas with them, as did Vanessa, Duncan, Clive and the children. There was little communication otherwise between the households for a number of years — apart from a wave of the hand when they passed each other on the track or met on walks.

One occasion when they did all meet was at a summer party at Tilton when, after a meal of grouse (three for eleven diners), there was an entertainment with, said Virginia in a letter to Lytton, 'a rustic audience'.

Maynard, she said, 'was crapulous and obscene beyond words, lifting his left leg and singing a song about Women'. Lydia, as Queen Victoria, danced to a bust of Albert. What, one wonders, did the yokels make of it?

Nigel Nicholson complained that Maynard and Lydia were 'remarkably economic in their hospitality', yet their erstwhile friends were only too ready to be lavishly entertained by them each Christmas. Maynard also organised a peace party at the end of the war when an effigy of Hitler was consumed on a bonfire.

So infrequently did the former friends meet in later years that when Vanessa met the couple while shopping in Lewes she did not at first recognise them. Maynard, who had suffered from angina since 1937, had become fat and unattractive, Lydia 'squat and insignificant'.

Maynard was created Baron Keynes of Tilton in 1942 and he died aged 62 at Tilton on Easter Sunday, 1946. Lydia stayed on at the house until 1977 when she moved to a nursing home in Seaford. She died there aged 89 in 1981.

Tilton is now privately owned — by Maynard's biographer Robert Skidelsky — and is not open to the public — nor is the track leading to the farmhouse.

ASHAM: THE END

O N Monday, September 1, 1919, the Woolfs moved out of Asham and into Monks House. Frank Gunn, the farm bailiff, provided two wagons to carry their furniture and effects across Southease Halt and the river bridge to Rodmell. Virginia stayed in London. 'It is very melancholy giving up this place,' she wrote to Roger Fry. 'Nothing will ever be like it; and Gunn is going to have every room painted, damn his soul! I shall haunt his wife and no doubt blast his first born.'

This photograph, from March 1991, shows Asham House boarded and desolate after decades of neglect
(Sussex Express and County Herald)

43

Asham House was put on the market five years later but the Woolfs, by then well established in Rodmell, decided not to buy it, and it was sold to a cement company that quarried the hill behind and to the side of the house, and built a huge processing plant between Asham and the river.

From Monks House Virginia and Leonard watched with horror and sadness as the elegant house was ravished. Heaps of spoil were dumped in the meadow which soon was covered with overgrown briars, bushes and trees.

Until the cement works closed in 1975 — when all the equipment and buildings were removed — Asham House was let to a succession of tenants. Later squatters moved in. The quarry, by then in the ownership of Blue Circle Industries, became a landfill site and, where once the trees and hedgerows around Asham had been coated with a white dust from the cement works, they were now festooned with windblown plastic as dustcarts disgorged their rubbish amid screaming, wheeling gulls. Just a few years before the only sound in the coombe had been the rooks cawing in the elms.

Had the Woolfs bought the property in 1924, when it was offered to them, the quarry would never have been excavated, the cement works that blighted a beautiful river valley for decades would not have been built, there would be no eyesore refuse dump and Asham House would still be standing. Would they have remained in Rodmell had they glimpsed the future?

Briefly, after the infilling of the quarry began, Asham was restored and used as a site manager's house, but it became uninhabitable as the piled-up waste edged nearer and seeping methane gas posed a hazard. Blue Circle wanted to increase the life of the tip (which, when filled, will be restored to natural Downland) by filling in the hollow where Asham House stood. In 1991 the company sought permission to demolish the listed property and rebuild it closer to the road. By then the house was beginning to fall apart; it had been vandalised and its mullioned windows were hidden behind rusting corrugated iron.

Moving the house proved not to be feasible and in 1994 Blue Circle sought and was given approval to demolish it in exchange for a financial package to benefit 'local heritage'.

Opposition continued until the eleventh hour. Melba Cuddy-Keane, president of the Virginia Woolf Society, said that history would be lost with the demolition of Asham. 'But at the same time another history will be made,' she added. 'Scholars of the future will study why and how Asham disappeared in the year 1994; it is the story of how tradition and scholarship lost the battle against economics and use. This will be our legacy for the twenty first century. We wish indeed we had been able to leave Asham to them instead.'

When Sussex Express reporter John Eccles visited the site in May 1994 just before the wreckers moved in, he wrote: 'The rooms are now threadbare and damp, but still have a vestige of grace. Rooks make a constant noise in the surrounding thick woods, also destined for removal. It is as if the area knows it is destined for destruction. And the shadow of Virginia Woolf looks forlornly down from an upstairs window.'

The French windows, two of the fireplaces and some of the garden tiles were salvaged for use elsewhere, and the house was pulled down in June 1994. Blue Circle offered a total of £626,000, to be divided between a Southdown Way walkers' bunkhouse at Asham, Charleston Farmhouse, a literary endowment, Monks House, Beddingham Church, Bloomsbury 'interpretation facilities', a Bloomsbury trail, materials salvage and a waste study.

The site of Asham House in October, 1994. Giant earthmovers prepare the valley for the twenty-first century's waste

(Sussex Express and County Herald)

Monks House, Rodmell, from the street

(Judy Moore)

LIFE AT MONKS HOUSE

AFTER the elegance and relative comfort of Asham, Monks House was primitive indeed — and small. The brick floors sweated, the house had no bathroom, no electricity, no hot water and no loo. Like the other villagers, the Woolfs made use of an earth privy in a grove of laurels in the garden with a cane chair placed over the bucket. Indoors they used chamber pots, emptied by their servants. Virginia told Lytton that there was charm in the place but compared to Asham it was unromantic.

Monks House is long and narrow, its ground floor above road level at the front and below the garden at the back. The Woolfs never used the front door, which leads straight into the former kitchen. Nor does the National Trust custodian who lives there now. The main entrance is through a full-length greenhouse on the south side. The low-ceilinged rooms are small, poky almost, and dark — made more so in the downstairs sitting room by the sea green walls Virginia favoured and the forest of greenery outside the windows.

It is an old building, believed to date from the fifteenth and sixteenth centuries, and listed as important historically and architecturally. Leonard and Virginia added a small east wing (sitting room upstairs, Virginia's bedroom downstairs) which is tacked incongruously on to the end of the cottage and which, today, would undoubtedly be refused planning permission. Interestingly, the new bedroom was not then, nor is it now, accessible from the house. Virginia had to go out into the garden and climb a flight of brick steps to reach the bedroom, whatever the weather.

A tiny cottage, Parsonage House, stood to the right of the entrance path until 1856, when it was pulled down. A year after moving in Leonard bought the site for £120 and made a lawn there. Later he converted it to the present paved garden with fish pond. The garden covered exactly one acre until Leonard bought the Pound Croft Field (where stray farm animals had been kept until reclaimed by their owners) in 1928 not only to extend the garden, but to prevent houses being built next to Monks House.

Initially Virginia was not happy with her weekend and holiday cottage in Rodmell and often thought of moving elsewhere when another house took her fancy. She considered Laughton Place, for which she was ready to 'pawn her shoelaces' and properties in Amberley, Alciston and elsewhere in Sussex. In 1925 she even thought of moving to the South of France. As improvements were made, though — inside plumbing, a new kitchen, the extension — she grew to love the house and its setting. 'Each day is . . . full of wandering clouds and that fading and rising of the light which so enraptures me in the downs!' she wrote.

When mist covered the valley she saw 'the village standing out to sea in the June night, houses seeming ships; the marsh a fiery foam'.

Before mains electricity was installed the Woolfs used Aladdin lamps. In September, 1929, they swapped their solid fuel range for an oil stove, and Virginia imagined the rich stews and the sauces she would cook, 'adventurous strange dishes with dashes of wine'.

Leonard was more interested in the garden than the house. He was an enthusiastic and knowledgeable horticulturalist, often too enthusiastic for his gardener, Percy Bartholomew. Percy's son, Jim, lives in a cottage overlooking Monks House. He knew the Woolfs from the time he was a baby. Leonard, he said, was always changing the layout of the garden, to Percy's despair. 'As soon as I get it straight he changes it again,' Percy used to complain.

Jim remembers the garden in its heyday when Leonard had three large greenhouses — 'Leonard's Crystal Palaces' Virginia called them — against the

The extension, seen from the garden. Above is a small sitting room, below Virginia's bedroom
(Judy Moore)

48

church path. Topiary was one of his enthusiams, cacti another, and fruit and flowers were grown for the house. At night he would go out with a lantern to catch and kill the slugs and snails attacking his vegetable crops and his prized blooms. As a boy Jim used to wheel barrows of anthracite to the greenhouses to fuel the furnaces. The orchard was beautifully mown then, there was a hazel copse on the churchyard boundary and six beehives. Old millstones from Rodmell Mill were set into the paths around the garden, and the Woolfs created a round pool designed to resemble a dewpond. But competing with the delicious flowery smells and the thyme scented breezes off the Downs was the always present odour of the cesspool.

A wooden shed, which Virginia called her writing lodge, stands at the end of the garden, its windows giving a view across the valley to Caburn. Before the shed was put up, Jim said, Virginia used a room below an old apple loft close to the house. Today the area is a flint walled courtyard with a magnificent magnolia and a lemon tree. The brick paving was the floor of the writing room, on which Virginia had rush matting. She kept a table in there and a Remington typewriter. An old fig that grew outside the loft is still flourishing.

In the thirties Percy tended four large vegetable gardens, and there were sweeping lawns to mow, endless brick paths to weed and terraces to lay — a big job for one man. Percy, who lived with his family across the village street in Park Cottages, earned £2 a week, a good wage then when his neighbouring farm labourers earned thirty shillings.

Leonard, a man of some obstinacy himself, often said that Percy was the most pig-headed man he knew, a characteristic which may have contributed to the battle of the peas and Percy's eventual downfall.

Virginia was very taken with Percy's wife Rose. 'She has been mad, squints and is singularly pure of soul' she wrote. Rose inherited £320 from an aunt and bought a set of big white teeth and a wireless. From time to time she helped out in the house and Virginia, sniffy about Rose's cooking, always warned visitors there would be nothing to eat when she was in the kitchen.

Said Jim: 'I liked Leonard. He was a nice man, the best of the Bloomsbury lot. I had a great deal of time for him.' Leonard was extremely kind to children, slipping Jim half a crown from time to time and taking baskets of fruit from the orchard into the school for the pupils.

'He was a shy, helpful man. He did things quietly and sensibly,' Jim said. 'I had the greatest respect for both of them; they were hard workers, professionals.'

When, many years later, Jim became chairman of Rodmell Parish Council, Leonard offered his services as parish clerk, in which capacity he served for seventeen years. He also offered Monks House for the council meetings. 'It was warmer than the village hall, and we didn't have to pay for it,' Jim explained.

Leonard, who was a manager of Rodmell Primary School, and president of

A view from the walled garden at Monks House towards Virginia's Woolf's writing lodge in the orchard
(Judy Moore)

Rodmell Horticultural Society for many years, had a sly sense of humour, according to Jim.

'He told obscure jokes that took you five minutes to work out. He was also an honourable man. Virginia was lucky to marry him and I think she knew it,' Jim said. 'When I was a boy I was in awe of him, but I ended up a friend of his.'

When the Woolfs were at their London house Percy used to prepare great hampers of fresh fruit and vegetables for them. The railway company sent a truck out from Lewes to pick up the hampers and put them on the London train. Percy's vegetables were known in the village for their size and succulence, helped, perhaps, by the contents of the cess pit which he emptied on them.

Like many of the Woolfs' friends, Jim found Monks House was often cold and damp, and always untidy with books and papers piled on the tables and desks. There were flowering geraniums, gloxinia and lilies in the windows and the pervading smell of cigarette smoke and woodsmoke, old bindings and apples.

Virginia's niece, Angelica, remembers the dining room as 'dimly green like a fish pond' with plants on the windowsills casting green light into the room. She described the atmosphere at Monks House as 'concentrated, quiet and mysterious'. Nigel Nicolson saw it as rambling, untidy, 'hugger-mugger' with books everywhere.

Virginia Woolf pictured at a family picnic at High and Over
(The Tate Gallery Archive, Vanessa Bell photographic collection, neg E21)

Leonard was a practical man. He tinkered with the car — Jim remembers a grey/green Lanchester — and maintained their Sunbeam bicycles. Virginia was quite the opposite — an indifferent cook (although she made excellent bread) and hopeless at housework.

Before the Lanchester the Woolfs had a Singer, bought second-hand in 1927 for £275, and most afternoons they hauled it out of the cowshed and ran it backwards up a bank because the engine jammed.

They motored all over the county for picnics and compared their car favourably with Maynard's secondhand Morris Cowley. They visited Arundel, Chichester and Rottingdean, Michelham Priory and Bodiam, often with the Bells, who had also bought a car. They especially enjoyed driving along the Esplanade at Seaford, fifty years and more before the beach was rebuilt to save the town from the long rollers that crashed against the crumbling sea wall, and sent cascades of water over passing cars.

Richard Kennedy's drawing of a Bloomsbury country walk, Virginia Woolf in the foreground, Mount Caburn in the background

(Drawing from *A Boy at The Hogarth Press*)

Virginia was very dependent on her servants, both in London and in the country. Annie Thompsett, who had a baby girl and was living on fifteen shillings a week, was her first cook/housekeeper at Rodmell. She was being turned out of the room she rented in the village and persuaded the Woolfs to buy her a cottage so she could stay there and work for them.

For £350 a cottage across the street from Monks House was acquired and from 1934 this was the home of Annie's successor, Louie Everest. Louie lived there rent free with her husband and two young children and was paid seven shillings and sixpence a week to work daily at Monks House from 8am to 9pm, with some free time in the afternoons. She stayed in this job until Leonard's death in 1969. In a published reminiscence Louie wrote that she was startled, while preparing breakfast, to hear Virginia apparently talking to herself in the bathroom above the kitchen. She was reassured by Leonard who explained that it was his wife's habit to speak aloud the sentences she had written to test their balance and sonority. Virginia wrote the most elegant, poetic prose — indeed one of the villagers told Leonard she had read all of his wife's books, even though she could not understand them, because the English was so beautiful.

The Woolfs were vigorous walkers, especially Virginia. After a morning of writing, and lunch, she would often walk to Piddinghoe where farmer Neville Gwynne's Jersey cows wore 'brown holland smocks', or through the hanging copses on the Downs.

Richard Kennedy, a boy apprentice at the Woolfs' Hogarth Press, went on a picnic and walk over the Downs with the Woolfs and Bells in 1928, and he recalled: 'LW stopped to have a pee in a very casual sort of way without attempting to have any sort of cover. I could see this was a part of his super-rational way of living'.

The writer and actor Dirk Bogarde, in *A Postillion Struck by Lightning*, the first volume of his autobiography, describes a boyhood fishing expedition with a couple of village characters, Reg and Perce, from his home near Alfriston.

They walked over Itford Hill, slithered down past Asham and crossed the railway line at Southease. Reg and Perce fished for pike and the boy lay back in the grass, bored 'until a lady came slowly walking across the field. She was tall and thin, with a long woolly, and fairish hair which looked rather wispy as if she had just washed it. She was carrying a walking stick and a bunch of wild flowers.

'Reg looked very grumpily at her and went on fishing. Perce just hunched his shoulders up and didn't move, which was very rude because she was smiling a little and looked quite kind.

'"Fishing?" she said in a silly way. Because what else could they be doing? Reg just looked at her and nodded his head, and Perce didn't do anything. "I think I'm lost. I can't find the bridge."' After the stranger had gone, stepping carefully over the tussocks and molehills, Perce said: '"Bloomin' nuisance her. She's always about when we get here. Always up and down the river she is, like a bloomin' witch".

"'A foreigner isn't she?" said Reg.

"'Londoner. From over there at Rodmell," said Perce, skewering the biggest grasshopper onto his hook. "They say she's a bit do-lally-tap . . . she writes books.'"

Sunday, Virginia thought, was the devil's own day in Rodmell, with children playing, barking from the garden next door where her neighbour Kathleen Emery bred fox terriers, and the church bells. In her diary she called them the 'cursed Xtian bells'. On another occasion she wrote that 'the Xtian religion' was 'silly and repulsive'.

In a letter to her sister in April, 1928, Virginia wrote: 'the Downs really are astonishing at this moment . . . but in 5 years we shall be driven out — theres no doubt of it'.

She had been walking along the river and found a race course on the flats by the railway halt, with stables and a stand 'run up from cheap wood'. The new owner of Southease Farm had started a pony racing course. At the same time she heard that thirty cottages were to be built across the river at Asham. 'Undoubtedly this country is doomed,' she wrote — but she did not have to move as both enterprises failed.

Another threat to the Woolfs' rural idyll was a plan to put a sewage pumping station in their field. Chailey Rural District Council, in August, 1938, proposed compulsory purchase of part of the field, but Leonard refused to sell and eventually the council backed down.

In the twenties there were eighty families living in Rodmell, half that of a generation previously, and Virginia saw it as a 'decaying village'. The young men were not taught farming and left for the towns, while old cottages were being bought for weekend retreats — as Monks House had been.

But there were always visitors — family and friends from Charleston came over for tea and friends arrived for the weekend or longer. They played bowls, croquet and archery in the garden and indulged in good conversation around the log fire in the evenings. Virginia would light a cheroot, bought from the Army and Navy Stores, after dinner, or smoke a hand-rolled cigarette made from My Mixture, which Richard Kennedy described as 'shag'. He remembered Virginia giving one to an American woman who nearly choked to death.

In his book, *A Boy at The Hogarth Press*, Kennedy wrote: 'She looks at us over the top of her steel-rimmed spectacles, her grey hair hanging over her forehead and a shag cigarette hanging form her lips.'

One visitor was Vita Sackville West, daughter of the third Baron Sackville and wife of diplomat Harold Nicolson. As Angus Davidson put it, Vita had a gift for intimate friendship with women and there was an instant attraction between her and Virginia. They described their friendship as sapphic. Virginia thought the aristocratic Vita rather glamorous — 'pink glowing, grape clustered, pearl hung' — and made her the model for the androgynous hero/heroine of her novel, *Orlando*. Her greatest asset, according to Virginia, were her legs 'running like slender pillars

Vanessa Bell, David Garnett, Virginia Woolf, Quentin Bell, Leonard Woolf and Angelica Bell with Leonard's spaniel Sally at Monks House

(The Tate Gallery Archive, Vanessa Bell photographic collection, neg Q38)

up into her trunk, which is that of a breastless cuirassier . . . but all about her is virginal, savage, patrician'.

Vita thought Virginia could not have been better named — 'a tenuousness and purity in her baptismal name and the hint of fang in her married name'.

During their three year affair Virginia was 'in the thick of the greatest rapture'. The two women visited each other often, Vita to Rodmell and Virginia to Long Barn in Kent, Vita's home before she moved to Sissinghurst Castle. They remained friends even when Vita moved to other relationships and Virginia became the object of Dame Ethel Smyth's passion. When they met in 1930 Virginia was forty-eight and Ethel, a writer, composer and militant suffragette, was seventy-two.

Leonard paid little attention to his wife's unorthodox liaisons. He had many other interests. He was a lifelong Socialist and encouraged the local branch of the Labour Party to meet at Monks House. The membership included Louie Everest, Mr Fears the postman, Mrs Larter the schoolmistress and writer Neil Lyons who lived in Southease. Virginia was amused, during the Abdication crisis in 1937, to find the members, considered red hot revolutionaries by the rest of the village, were more interested in the affairs of the king and Wallis Simpson than the minutes of the last meeting and matters arising.

Leonard was careful with money, concerned that they should earn enough to cover the costs of their two homes. But he was always generous to children — with half crowns for the gardener's son and, years later, crisp ten shilling notes for his wife's great nephew Julian Bell.

An interesting light is thrown on their financial arrangements by this entry in Virginia's diary on January 3, 1936: 'L says I have not made enough to pay my share of the house & have to find £70 out of my hoard'.

However, there were funds enough, two years later, to bring in Lewes builder Percy Wicks to make a library for Leonard in the roof space. A gabled dormer window was installed, and a second window was inset into the roof, with a little balcony where they sat on summer evenings.

CHARLESTON: THE THIRTIES

THE thirties decade was marked by professional success and personal tragedy for the artists at Charleston. In 1931 Duncan's first lover, Lytton Strachey, died and a few weeks later Dora Carrington killed herself. Vanessa's one-time lover and faithful friend, Roger Fry, died in 1934. Strangely enough their relationship was not referred to by Virginia Woolf, usually an astute observer of the sexual scene, in her biography of her sister.

Charleston Farmhouse — a view from the walled garden. The French doors on the right lead to Vanessa Bell's bedroom and Duncan Grant's studio

(Judy Moore)

On the artistic front this was a time of achievement for Vanessa and Duncan — a man for whom the Oxfam shops might have been invented, such was the chaos of his wardrobe. They had, in a way, joined the art establishment for their work was recognised, they exhibited and received commissions.

In 1935 Duncan was asked to paint three panels for the main lounge of RMS *Queen Mary*. Vanessa was commissioned to produce a panel for one of the private sitting rooms on the liner and the Cunard-White Star Company asked them both to advise on interior colour schemes, carpets and fabrics.

When Duncan's panels were completed the company chairman, Sir Percy Bates, refused them. They were, he declared, unsuitable for his clientele.

The London art world was outraged at what it considered an act of commercial philistinism and such was the rumpus whipped up in the press that the company was obliged not only to pay Duncan his fee but to pay him compensation as well.

There was trouble, too, with Vanessa's panel, destined for a room next to the ship's Roman Catholic chapel. The church authorities found her design 'offensive' and her contract was cancelled. Maynard intervened and Vanessa was re-employed to produce a panel for a private dining room.

The household moved between London, Charleston and Cassis. When in France they pre-empted the single market economy by buying barrels of wine from Chateau Fontcreuse and shipping them home to bottle for their cellar in Sussex.

Among those entertained at Charleston in this period was Julian's Cambridge friend, Anthony Blunt, who was to become Surveyor of the Queen's Pictures, head of the Courtauld Institute and to receive a knighthood.

They had become friends as fellow Apostles at Cambridge and Julian confessed to his mother that they had slept together. Years later Blunt was exposed as a Soviet agent years later and named as the 'fourth man' in the Burgess-Maclean-Philby story of treachery and defection.

In 1935, Julian, an essayist and poet, was appointed professor of English at Wu-Han University in China. Vanessa drove him to Newhaven where he caught the ferry for Dieppe to begin his journey east.

His contract was for three years but he did not complete it as he became romantically involved with the Chinese wife of a colleague and considered it prudent to resign. He left China in 1937 intending to fight for the International Brigade in Spain but the family prevailed upon him to volunteer his services as an ambulance driver rather than as a fighter. Julian agreed and in June he left with his ambulance, again from Newhaven, his mother waving to him from the quayside. It was the last time she was to see her son for, a few weeks later, on July 18, Julian was hit by a shell fragment and died of his wounds.

Vanessa never fully recovered from the death of her firstborn. She was in London when the news came and was taken, prostrate with grief, to Charleston. In the days, weeks and months that followed she was inconsolable. Virginia drove over from Rodmell daily when she was in Sussex and showered her sister with letters of love and comfort. 'When Vanessa faced the depths of despair and doubted her existence it was to Virginia to whom she turned,' wrote Jane Dunn in *A Very Close Conspiracy*.

Clive Bell pictured on the terrace at Charleston

(The Tate Gallery Archive, Vanessa Bell photographic collection, neg B25)

Firle church

(Judy Moore)

ANOTHER WAR

WHEN Quentin was found to have tuberculosis it proved a blessing in one way as he was declared unfit for military service when Britain went to war with Germany again in 1939. Instead he was employed by Maynard on farm work at Tilton and, together with his father, Clive, he joined the Home Guard. At the outbreak of war Vanessa and Duncan moved back to Charleston 'for the duration' but it was to be their permanent home for the rest of their lives.

Bunny's prophecy of scandal at Angelica's birth was fulfilled in 1940 when she announced she was in love with him — her father's former lover. Angelica was twenty one, and had been informed of her true parentage, in the garden room at Charleston, four years earlier. She was not, however, told of her father's involvement with Bunny, her senior by twenty-six years and with a wife, Ray Marshall, who was dying of cancer.

Angelica's announcement caused fresh anguish for Vanessa. The family considered the relationship 'grotesque' and in what must have been a bizarre encounter, Duncan summoned Bunny to Charleston and asked his intentions towards his daughter.

Shortly after the death of his wife in March, 1940, Bunny and Angelica moved to Claverham Farm at Berwick which they had rented for nine months. Later they married but Vanessa and Duncan were not invited to the wedding and the relationship between mother and her daughter remained cool for many months. The couple subsequently had four children, all girls, and today Angelica, a widow, lives in the south of France.

Virginia's suicide in 1941 was another catastrophic blow for Vanessa, who was still mourning the loss of her son. The Woolfs' gardener, Percy Bartholomew, telephoned with the news that Virginia was missing and Vanessa hurried to Rodmell but there was nothing she could do, nor did Leonard want her there. Angelica cycled to Charleston from Claverham to be with her mother and Duncan rushed down from London. Distraught, the family clung to one another.

The early years of the war brought personal tragedy to Charleston but it did not put a stop to the artistic activity of its occupants. Duncan spent two months as a war artist at Portsmouth where he had a chance to meet some attractive young sailors. On his return he and Vanessa met the two elderly sisters who had moved from

Northease Manor, near Rodmell, to Millers, a house on St Anne's Hill in Lewes, and opened an art gallery there.

Mrs Frances Byng Stamper and Miss Caroline Byng Lucas, known as Bay and Mouie, were wards of Princess Marie-Louise and had been brought up in royal circles. Each week they would travel to London to use their ration cards at Fortnum and Mason, at the same time securing the works of Rodin, Degas and Henry Moore for exhibition in Lewes. They devoted one of the shows to an Omega retrospective and another to the paintings of Duncan and Vanessa. They also instituted a series of lectures given by prominent people in the art world, and it became the custom for them to lunch with their friends from Charleston at the White Hart or Shelleys Hotel in Lewes before these lectures.

The grey-on-grey stencilled Paisley pattern wallpaper for the garden room at Charleston was created by Vanessa after the war ended. At the same time she and Duncan hand painted black and grey geometric wallpaper for the dining room and they made a south facing patio with inset mosaic patterns formed with broken crockery and glass at the far end of the walled garden. They also resumed their painting holidays in Europe, although they no longer had Cassis.

It was in 1946 Duncan that met the poet and writer Paul Roche, who was to become a dominant figure in the later years of his life. When he first saw Paul, whom he called Don, in Piccadilly Circus, the young man was newly out of a seminary and attached to St Mary's Roman Catholic Church in Chelsea. He was dressed as a sailor and it was many months before Duncan discovered he was not in the Navy. Duncan, then 61, took Paul home to see his pictures — and so began a friendship that was to last more than thirty years.

Encouraged by Duncan, Paul left the church and began to write. Duncan painted countless pictures of the young man and wanted him to move in to Charleston. Although Paul was heterosexual, Vanessa saw him as a serious threat to her, by then, serene, untroubled country life and she made it clear he would not be welcome.

Paul, who considered that Vanessa held Duncan back from becoming an artist of the first rank, was aware of her fear of him and only rarely visited Sussex during her lifetime.

In 1954 he left for America with his fiancee, Clarissa, but kept in constant touch with Duncan. When Vanessa died Duncan wired him — 'Vanessa dead, come back' — and Paul returned to devote the next two decades to his old friend, giving up his work to care for him in his last year. In return Duncan paid him a small salary and made him his principal heir.

Adrian Stephen died in 1948, leaving Vanessa, eldest of the four Stephen children, the only one surviving. She took comfort in her later years from her grandchildren — Angelica's girls Amaryllis, Henrietta, Nerissa and Fanny, and the

Duncan Grant photographed in his studio at Charleston on his 90th birthday

(Anthony Tree)

children of Quentin and his wife Anne Olivier Popham, the art histórian, whom he married in 1952. Quentin was then lecturing in art education at King's College, Newcastle.

The children spent idyllic summers at Charleston. Amaryllis and Henrietta, draped in an assortment of old fabrics, posed for their grandparents, listened to family stories and to *Mrs Dale's Diary* on the radio. They charged Vanessa and Duncan modelling fees of sixpence an hour .

As she grew older Vanessa, who had a successful operation for breast cancer in a Hove nursing home in 1944, was plagued with rheumatism but she enjoyed playing with her grandchildren, and making dolls' clothes.

At 11.30am on April 17, 1961, when she was 81, she died of double pleurisy at Charleston, twenty years and ten days after Virginia killed herself. Five days later Duncan, Quentin, Angelica and Grace accompanied her coffin to Firle churchyard where she was buried. There was no service, and a plain black tombstone, carrying only her name and dates, was erected. Clive, in hospital in London with a broken leg, was unable to be there.

Duncan remained at Charleston, travelling abroad each year with friends until he was in his nineties. Grace, the 'angel of Charleston' retired and the household was run by a couple from Firle. The house fell into a state of disrepair and encroaching weeds covered the garden. On a visit Paul found canvases carelessly

Duncan Grant at an exhibition of his work at Rye Art Gallery, Rye, May 1977. From the left, Paul Roche, Richard Schone, Russell Scott, Duncan Grant, Barbara Bagenal

(Sussex Express and County Herald)

The gravestones of Duncan Grant, left, and Vanessa Bell, right, in Firle churchyard
(Judy Moore)

stacked in mouldering heaps, scratched with nail marks because they had not been hammered into the stretchers properly. One painting had been lodged in a broken window to keep out the rain and another was being used as an oil rag. This painting he straightened out, framed and sold 'for good honest cash' at Heals.

In October, 1977, Duncan, frail and senile, moved from Charleston to The Stables at Aldermaston to live with Paul and his family. He died there on May 9, 1978, aged 93, of bronchial pneumonia, and was buried in the churchyard at Firle next to Vanessa.

Quentin and his wife, Angelica, Grace and Walter, Angus Davidson and the Roches were at the burial. On June 27 a memorial service was held at St Paul's Cathedral in London.

WAR YEARS IN RODMELL

IN August 1939 Leonard and Virginia changed their London address, moving from Tavistock Square to a flat in Mecklenburgh Square. When war was declared they decided to follow Vanessa, Clive and Duncan's example and move to Sussex for the duration. The car was taken to have its headlights hooded; Virginia sewed blackout curtains; and found, when she cycled to Lewes for provisions at Flints, that the shop was almost empty. People, remembering the shortages of the First World War only a generation earlier, had bought up all the groceries they could get.

Evacuees from Bermondsey arrived in Rodmell, but within a week or two most had returned to London, shocked by living conditions in the countryside.

Virginia was concerned about earning enough money to survive the war. She economised on paper, stinted on sugar and butter, hoarded candles and matches.

The first winter of the war was Arctic, the hardest in living memory. The great frost lasted from December 22 to February 4, and the temperature plummeted to ten degrees Fahrenheit — twenty-two below freezing. The sea, and the tidal Ouse, froze over. During the night of January 27–28 frozen rain fell, coating everything with a thick, icy glaze. Each blade of grass, each twig, each leaf was encased. Birds were frozen by their feet to the branches, sheep were frozen by their wool to gorse bushes on the Downs.

Monks House, heated only by log fires, and always damp, was decidedly uncomfortable for a couple accustomed to the warmth of their London home in winter. They had to cook on a coal fire when the oil ran out and resorted to candles and their old Aladdin lamps when the power lines were brought down. They did not wash and slept in stockings and mufflers. 'Never was there such a medieval winter,' Virginia noted. The snow blew into her bedroom and the door hinges froze.

There was consternation in the village when Neville Gwynne, who farmed at Piddinghoe, tried to stop people collecting fallen twigs and branches from his woods to fuel their fires. He was soundly berated by Mr Paul, the tenant farmer at Southease, who claimed local people had a right to collect kindling.

For much of February and March, 1940, Virginia suffered from influenza and bronchitis but she recovered in the spring and began to take an interest in village affairs. Leonard was on fire watching and air raid precaution duties. He and his team used to practice with an ancient wheeled pump, pulled by four men, but they were called out in earnest only once when an incendiary bomb set a haystack alight.

There were first aid sessions and a lecture in the village hall on how charcoal absorbs gas. They handed in their aluminium saucepans to be made into aeroplanes and Virginia joined Rodmell Women's Institute and was elected treasurer.

The threat of invasion was never far from their thoughts and in May they discussed suicide if the Germans came. They feared that Leonard, a Jew, would be tortured and incarcerated. They had enough petrol stored in the garage to kill themselves by carbon monoxide poisoning and Adrian had supplied them with a lethal dose of morphine each. Adrian himself planned suicide in the event of invasion and, according to Leonard, Harold and Vita had also provided themselves with a similar 'bare bodkin'. But within days Virginia was writing in her diary that she did not want the garage to see the end of her, and that she wanted ten more years.

Leonard became engrossed in his garden, creating a rockery that spring. He lectured for the Workers' Education Association and continued to host meetings of Rodmell Labour Party in the dining room.

A pill box, a six sided brick structure, with slits for guns, was built in the field next to Monks House. It was one of a series all up the Ouse Valley. The boxes were provisioned for three days and manned by the Local Defence Volunteers (later the Home Guard), who were required to engage any German invaders in battle.

On her afternoon perambulations Virginia saw the hospital ships arrive in Newhaven, laden with wounded as the enemy pushed the British Expeditionary Force back to the Channel ports, and from their garden she and Leonard watched the long hospital trains taking the wounded up the line to Lewes and beyond.

The WI prevailed upon Virginia to allow play rehearsals to be held in Monks House. Her contribution to the war, she wrote, was the sacrifice of pleasure.

'I'm bored: bored and appalled by the ready made commonplaceness of those plays; which they cant act unless we help. I mean, the minds so cheap, compared with ours, like a bad novel — thats my contribution — and have my mind smeared by the village and WEA mind: & to endure it, & to simper'.

Her upbringing had not equipped Virginia to understand the lower orders and she was struck by their helplessness. When she heard that the young Duke of Northumberland had fallen in the war she considered it 'a kind of crash . . . for a duke to fall, compared with a Harry West' (Louie's brother). She could be cruel and thoughtless to people who were 'not one's own kind'. She sacked Nellie Boxall, when she became old, ill and unable to work as before, and she marvelled at the 'bloodless servitude of the domestic poor'.

The evacuation of Dunkirk began on May 26 and again the Woolfs had a serious debate about suicide. They feared it would be only a matter of days before the invasion began. During June and July there were nightly air raids on the south and

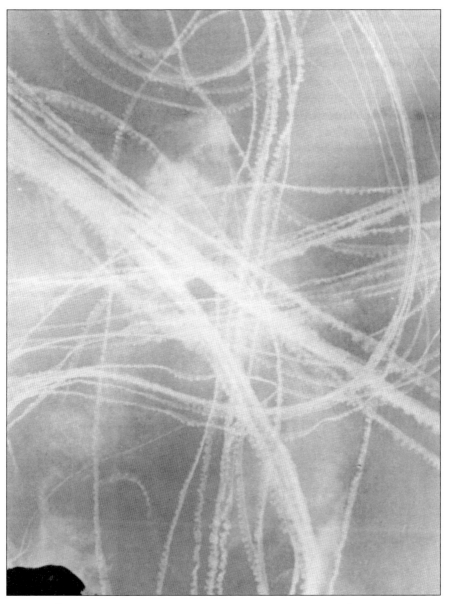

Vapour trails of The Few above the Ouse Valley during the Battle of Britain; the ramparts of Lewes Castle bottom left

(Edward Reeves)

east coasts of England, and above the Ouse Valley after dark searchlights swept the sky trying to pinpoint enemy planes. 'It's rather lovely about 2 in the morning to see the lights stalking the Germans over the marshes', Virginia wrote to John Lehmann.

That was the summer of the Battle of Britain when Britain's young airmen, some barely out of school, took to the skies to repel the enemy above Kent and Sussex. The Woolfs saw both British and German planes shot down — at Tarring Neville, over Lewes racecourse and on Caburn, where a Messerchmitt crashed 'like a settled moth, wings extended'.

They were in the garden during a raid on August 16, and lay flat on their faces beneath a tree, their hands behind their heads. Leonard told Virginia not to close her teeth, sound advice for a bomb fell close by, rattling the windows of the house and her writing lodge. In September 1940 the banks of the Ouse were breached by a bomb intended for the cement works, and the water meadows flooded. A few days later, during an abnormally high tide, a huge stretch of river bank collapsed and flood waters reached right up to the village and north to Caburn, which stood like a cliff above a great lake. The bridge at Southease was cut off and Denny Botten's haystacks appeared to float on a vast expanse of water.

Virginia wrote to Angelica of her infinite delight in the cascades of water roaring over the meadows. 'All the gulls came and rode the waves at the end of the field.'

Their former London home in Tavistock Square was bombed, so was the Mecklenburgh Square flat, and they had to rescue what remained of their furniture, books and possessions and transport them to Sussex. They inquired about renting Yew Tree House in Lewes, at a cost of £110 a year, for storage, but settled instead on taking rooms in Botten's farmhouse. Carvills of Lewes charged them £25 to convey their salvaged home to Rodmell but when the farmer saw the load he allowed the Woolfs only two of his rooms instead of three 'because of the inflammable furniture'. Their books were sent to a store room in Mill House, higher up the village.

There was an Indian summer in 1940 and Virginia picked and stored apples and collected combs from Leonard's beehives. She decanted twenty jars of honey and in the evenings she occupied herself with a new hobby — rug making. Vita sent wool from her Jacob sheep at Sissinghurst Castle, enough for Virginia to knit a jersey for herself and socks for Leonard. 'Two old Wolves dressed in real sheep's clothing' said Louie.

Police Constable Collins called from time to time to complain about defects in the blackout. Virginia's curtains did not fit too well but she was never prosecuted even at a time when each week the Sussex Express reported the court cases and fines of other householders who had not observed the strict blackout regulations. She showed no gratitude to the village bobby. She found him rude and offensive, bullying and threatening, glad to 'give a lady a bit of his mind'. The working class, she wrote, had no manners to fall back on.

As Britain stood alone against the might of the Third Reich that winter the hardships increased. Rations were tightened, there was little in the shops, prices rose and new clothes were a thing of the past. Like everyone else Leonard and Virginia had to make do and mend. They found it increasingly difficult to maintain the level of hospitality they had always offered at Monks House. 'It takes thought and trouble to feed one extra,' Virginia wrote.

There were no turkeys to be had for Christmas 1940, and the Woolfs made do with a duck. Occasionally Vanessa supplied them with eggs from the Charleston chickens, and Dr Octavia Wilberforce (great grand-daughter of the slave emancipator William Wilberforce, and also distantly related to the Stephen family) sent milk and cream by train from her West Sussex farm.

On Christmas Eve 1940 Virginia noted that her hand was becoming palsied, and after Christmas she fought against a rising tide of depression.

By March she was seriously unwell. She felt she was going mad and this time would not recover. On March 27, Leonard took her to Dr Wilberforce's surgery in Montpelier Crescent, Brighton, but it was too late.

The view from the cockpit of a German Dornier 17 bomber over the Ouse Valley water meadows on Sunday, August 18, 1940. Centre left the railway halt at Southease and top right the cement works close to Asham House. Rodmell is just out of shot to the right

(From *Battle Over Sussex* by Pat Burgess and Andy Saunders)

69

The banks of the River Ouse where Virginia Woolf drowned herself in March, 1941. On the hill opposite is the scar of the chalk quarry above Asham House

(Judy Moore)

THE LAST WALK

IT is a longish walk from Monks House to the banks of the River Ouse and when she set out across the water meadows on the morning of March 28, 1941, Virginia Woolf took her walking stick to help her over the tussocky ground.

She had left letters for her husband and her sister on a table in the upstairs sitting room, and her cook saw her striding quickly up the garden to the top gate.

Beyond the cottage a wide view of the river valley in the encircling Downs opens up beneath a vast sky which, just a few months before Virginia's last walk, had been a backdrop to screaming aerial dog fights as Britain's young pilots — The Few — fought and won the Battle of Britain.

There is a great quietness in the wide valley. Cloud shadows chase across the sheep-scattered Downs, Friesians amble through lush meadows, golden in summer with buttercups, and small, fat, Thelwell ponies frolic in paddocks over towards Iford. The scene was not so peaceful then. In 1941 towering steel poles, linked by wires, marched across the water meadows to prevent German gliders from landing, and there was the ugly cement factory blocking the view of melancholy Asham House, its tall chimney belching a white dust that coated the trees and hedgerows. In a letter to Lytton Strachey in September, 1927, Virginia had written: 'They are starting a cement works at Asheham. A railway line runs round the field, and the down behind is nothing but chalk. Isn't it damnable?'

Perhaps Virginia strode purposefully, intent only on ending her pain; perhaps she lingered for a last glimpse of Lewes Castle on its bosky prominence, or the strange low mound where Norman monks made their coney warren.

That bright spring morning she would have heard birdsong, and the whispering of reeds in the brooks criss-crossing the meadows. She may have looked over to Caburn, the landmark framed by the window of her writing lodge, though its Celtic fields, delineated only by the slanting evening sun, would have been invisible to her.

Virginia walked on over the rough grass and when she reached the river and searched for heavy stones to fill her pockets she found herself almost opposite Asham. Did she look beyond the clangorous wharf, linked to the cement works by aerial ropeway along which swung buckets of coal and sacks of cement, to the crater of a chalk quarry scarring the slope where she and Leonard had walked their dogs and hunted for mushrooms on misty autumn mornings?

Three weeks later a group of boys playing near Glynde Reach, an arm of the tidal Ouse to the north east, found Virginia's body floating in the water.

Today, a farm track from the bottom of the village street leads out across the water meadows to the river. Pilgrims following Virginia Woolf's last sad journey are often seen setting off through a copse of sycamores and willows, rowans and hawthorns, with a crystal brook babbling along beside the track. Beyond the brook the wartime pillbox still stands.

Jim Bartholomew's mother, Rose, always maintained that Virginia had attempted suicide earlier in March when she had come upon her returning from the river covered in mud.

Jim was at war in a minesweeper then, but his sister told him what had happened on March 28. She, Percy and Rose had just sat down to their midday meal when Leonard burst in, crying 'Percy, come quickly'.

He had spent the morning gardening and been summoned by the lunch bell at 1pm. Virginia did not appear and Leonard told Louie he was popping upstairs for a few minutes to hear the BBC news on the radio. Louie remembered him running back down the stairs, saying that something had happened to Virginia.

He ran to fetch Percy, who summoned the policeman, and all three hurried over the meadows to the river bank. There they found Virginia's walking stick standing in the mud, and footprints leading into the water.

The men searched across the brooks and in the village, giving up only when darkness fell. Vanessa had been summoned by Percy, but Leonard sent her home. He wanted to be alone.

From The Sussex Express and County Herald, April 4, 1941:
'Novelist's Disappearance
Mrs. Virginia Woolf
of Rodmell
'Mrs. Virginia Woolf, the well-known novelist, disappeared last Friday from her home, Monks House, Rodmell, and no trace has yet been found of her.

'It is generally believed that she fell into the river at Rodmell while out walking, and arrangements are being made to drag the river.

'Her husband, Mr. Leonard Woolf, has not been able to give the police much information regarding his wife's disappearance, and no clue has been found.

'Mrs. Woolf, who was 58, was the author of nearly a score of books. She gained the Prix Femina for the best English novel by a woman writer with the book "To the Lighthouse", published in 1927. She was well known in Rodmell and district, as also is her husband.'

Virginia's body was found on April 18 and Leonard was called to identify it. The cremation was in Brighton on April 21. Only Leonard was present, and he buried her ashes in the garden of Monks House beneath one of the two great interlaced elms which they had named Leonard and Virginia.

The last words of her book, *The Waves,* are her epitaph: 'Against you I will fling myself, unvanquished and unyielding, O Death'. On April 24 1941 the Sussex Express and County Herald, beneath a four-deck headline:

'Authoress's Last Note —

"A Feeling I shall Go Mad"

MRS VIRGINIA WOOLF'S BODY IN

RIVER NEAR HER RODMELL HOME

carried this story:

"'I have a feeling I shall go mad in these terrible times," is part of a note left by Mrs. Virginia Woolf, the well-known authoress, of Monks House, Rodmell, whose body was found in the River Ouse near her home on Friday. She disappeared on the morning of March 28th. At an inquest at Newhaven on Saturday, Dr E F Hoare (Coroner for East Sussex) recorded a verdict of "suicide while the balance of her mind was disturbed".

'Mrs. Woolf was seen on the river bank at 11.40 on the morning she vanished. When the body was found it was seen that her wristlet watch had stopped at 11.54. There was a large stone in one of the coat pockets.

'Mr. Leonard Sidney Woolf, the husband, said he last saw his wife at about 11 o'clock on the morning of March 28th. She had said she would leave the housework and go for a walk. Later he found two notes in her handwriting. One was addressed to him and one to her sister, Mrs. Bell. After he had read the note addressed to him he went along the river bank, where he found his wife's walking stick and saw footprints in the mud.

'The note read by the Coroner stated: "I have a feeling I shall go mad in these terrible times. I hear voices and cannot concentrate on my work. I have fought against it, but cannot fight any longer. You have always been so perfectly good to me. I owe all my happiness in life to you and I cannot go on and spoil your life." The Coroner said the other note was of a similar character and referred to the fact that she "could not fight against it any longer".

'Continuing his evidence, Mr. Woolf said that the day before his wife disappeared he was so concerned about her health that he phoned a doctor friend to come and see her. At first she refused to see him, saying it was all so hopeless. Witness had always been very anxious about her. She was highly strung and latterly she had been very depressed. In 1917 and 1918 she had nervous breakdowns, and on each occasion there had been a fear that she would take her life.

'Mr. J.C. Hubbard, of Rodmell, said he was working near the river bank on the morning of March 28th.' At 11.40 he saw Mrs. Woolf, but he did not notice her go to the river.

By the Coroner — Mrs. Woolf frequently went for a walk along the river banks, but it was mostly in the afternoons and rarely in the mornings. P.C. Collins said he found the body at about 1.30 on Friday afternoon in the River Ouse about two miles north of the cement wharf.

'The Coroner said there was no shadow of doubt that the lady's mind was unbalanced when she did the act. She had a history of a certain nervous disposition, she had an extremely sensitive nature. She was much more responsive than most people to the general beastliness that was happening in the world today.'

In the margin of a second letter Virginia left for Leonard she asked him to destroy all her papers. What exactly she meant by 'all' is unclear. Leonard did not destroy the twenty-six volumes of her diary, her letters or the manuscript of her last book, *Between the Acts*, completed just before her death. It has been called the longest suicide note in the English language. Virginia thought it 'silly and trivial'. She believed she had lost the ability to write and that the madness was closing in on her. When *Between the Acts* was published posthumously it was acclaimed as a masterpiece.

Leonard spent most of the rest of the war years in London, moving from patched up rooms in Mecklenburgh Square to a flat in Cliffords Inn then to a house in Victoria Square, which he kept until his death. He sold his equity in the Hogarth Press to Chatto and Windus for whom, coincidentally, Jim Bartholomew became a book jacket designer after the war.

Louie and Percy continued to be employed at Monks House until the incident of the peas — although Leonard, in his autobiography, made no mention of it, maintaining that Percy left his employ when he became blind.

Jim Bartholomew explained: 'Professional gardeners have a code. They will supply the kitchen with vegetables, but won't allow the kitchen to help itself. The cook did. She went out and picked the peas. Dad went in and told her off, she complained to Leonard and Dad was summoned.

'"Percy, you'll have to go," said Leonard, and Dad went.' 'That was the way it used to be,' said Jim's wife Mary. 'Good cooks were harder to find than good gardeners, and you looked after your cook!'

In his later years Leonard, still working as a journalist, co-editor of *Political Quarterly*, and a director of the *New Statesman*, found new companionship with the artist Trekkie Parsons, who was born in South Africa in 1902. She was the wife of Ian Parsons, a director of Chatto and Windus, and the couple had a summer home in neighbouring Iford. Their London home was in the same street as Leonard's and after the war the Parsons moved in with Leonard in Victoria Square.

Trekkie divided her time between Ian and Leonard, and at Monks House Leonard doubled the size of Virginia's writing lodge for Trekkie to use as a studio. He travelled extensively, back to Ceylon where he had been a civil servant in his youth, to the United States, Israel and Europe, often with Trekkie.

In 1969 Louie, who by then had been working at Monks House for thirty six years, had to go to hospital in Brighton for an operation. Leonard, over eighty, visited her every day. She returned home and was still recuperating when Leonard

Leonard Woolf in the garden of Monks House with his dogs
(Jim Bartholomew)

suffered a stroke. An ambulance was called but Louie sent it away, knowing that Leonard would not want to go to hospital.

Instead the doctor came and Louie and a neighbour cared for him until two nurses were hired. He died on August 14 and his ashes were buried under the second elm by the pond. Virginia's elm fell, later, in a gale, and Leonard's succumbed to Dutch elm disease.

Bust of Virginia Woolf by Stephen Tomlin in the garden of Monks House
(Judy Moore)

Bust of Leonard Woolf by Charlotte Hewes in the garden of Monks House
(Judy Moore)

In the garden at Monks House are two cast lead portrait busts, that of Virginia by Stephen Tomlin (the original bust is at Charleston) and Leonard's by Charlotte Hewes. Beneath Leonard's bust are the words: 'I believe profoundly in two rules, justice and mercy. They seem to me the foundation of all civilised life and society if you include under mercy toleration'.

So carefully preserved is the interior — matches and tobacco laid casually on a table, a book by a chair, geraniums in the window — that the visitor feels that at any moment Leonard may come in from the garden, scraping the mud off his boots and reaching for his pipe, or Virginia will return from one of her afternoon strolls down the valley.

The furnishings are eclectic. There are some fine pieces, furniture from the Omega Workshops, tables and chairs a secondhand dealer would reject. Saul Bellow planned to rent Monks House in the seventies, but when he saw how primitive it was even then, after the extensions and the installation of electricity and plumbing, he turned it down.

The house is administered by the National Trust and cared for by a resident custodian. It is open on Wednesday and Saturday afternoons from 2pm from April 1 to the end of October.

CHARLESTON TODAY

AFTER Duncan's death the house was found to be in a state of total decay, and it was taken over by what was to become the Charleston Trust. The restorers were thorough, yet restrained. The old building was made safe and dry, the hand painted wallpapers were carefully removed while the walls were repaired, then restored and re-hung, and especially-commissioned Bloomsbury fabrics, made by Laura Ashley, were used to re-cover some of the chairs. Yet this massive undertaking by the Trust is invisible, as was intended, and the interior today is as it was before Vanessa's death, none too tidy, a little shabby, cosy and comfortable.

Quentin Bell pictured in front of Charleston Farmhouse in July 1979 before restoration work began
(Sussex Express and County Herald)

Notices on a background of Charleston grey direct visitors up a mile of farm track to the farmhouse. It is isolated and peaceful, the only sounds the song of birds and an occasional passing tractor. There is a rich country smell compounded of cattle, silage and Downland herbage.

In front of the house is a large, willow bordered pond where waterfowl dart in and out of the reeds. To the side is an old walled garden where cottage garden flowers jostle for space with fruit and vegetables. At the far end is the mosaic patio — something of a disappointment as the carefully arranged pottery and glass shards are set in a decaying concrete. Prolific fig trees take the warmth from mellow old walls and a cascading vine creates a shady arbour outside the painters' studio.

Unexpectedly, the facade is not the golden stone portrayed in Vanessa Bell's 1950 painting *Charleston Farmhouse*. Rather it has a grey cement render while the south side is pebble dashed and the north, facing the walled garden, has a recent faux stone render. Together these different finishes combine to give the typical Sussex farmhouse a rather strange and unorthodox appearance.

Inside it is even stranger. Instead of the usual oak country furniture, old beams, plain walls, gleaming brass and copper in such houses, Charleston is ablaze with colour. Wherever a surface presented itself — walls and fireplace surrounds, shelves, door panels, furniture, ceiling beams — the artists decorated it.

Juxtaposed with painted pieces from the Omega Workshops are priceless antiques — a massive marquetry table in the study, given to Vanessa and Clive as a wedding present; an heirloom cabinet in the studio handed down to Vanessa from William Makepeace Thackeray's family; a display cabinet in the dining room from Vanessa's parents' home — and cheap junk shop finds transformed into works of art. In an outbuilding where a film about Bloomsbury is shown to visitors there is even a bottled-gas heater which has been decorated Bloomsbury style.

Charleston's gardens and grounds were restored in 1987 as a gift of Lila Acheson Wallace, co-founder of *Reader's Digest*.

The house is open to the public from 2pm to 6pm Wednesday to Sunday, and Bank Holiday Monday, from April to October, and from 11am Wednesday to Saturday from the second week in July to the end of August. The kitchen is open on Thursday and Friday only.

In November and December the house is open on Saturday and Sunday, 2pm to 5pm, selected rooms only, at reduced charge. A converted barn across the track serves as a visitor centre where Duncan Grant duvet covers, Vanessa Bell needlepoint kits, Grace Higgens' cookery book, postcards, pictures and Charleston-grown plants may be bought.

A programme of pottery exhibitions runs from April to October and there is an annual Charleston Arts Festival. The Charleston International Summer School each year includes visits to Knole and Rodmell. For details call the administrator on 01323 811265.

BERWICK CHURCH

THE Bloomsbury Trail in Sussex ends in the tiny twelfth-century church of St Michael and All Angels at Berwick, its walls adorned by murals painted by Duncan Grant, Vanessa Bell and her son, Quentin.

The leaded windows of this little church had been replaced with plain glass when they were shattered by a wartime bomb blast. As a result the interior was lighter and brighter — and eminently suitable as a place in which to revive the tradition of wall painting in Sussex churches. This was a project dear to the heart of that forward looking patron of ecclesiastical art, the Rt Rev George Bell, Bishop of Chichester from 1929 to 1958.

'Old churches must serve a living purpose,' he said, 'and in doing so necessary changes must be introduced. They have survived, and will only continue to survive, when used for the purpose for which they were intended. The contributions already made to the structure and adornment of their interiors are equally of historic value. Why should not the present age also make its contribution?'

It was architect, Sir Charles Reilly, who suggested that Duncan Grant should be commissioned to make a mid-twentieth century contribution to the interior of St Michael and All Angels. Duncan proposed a joint scheme with Vanessa Bell, a fellow member of the Society of Mural Painters, and Quentin.

The parochial church council considered the scheme and, despite opposition from some members, approved it in May 1941. A church advisory committee also recommended that a faculty be granted — on condition an architectural adviser were appointed. The man chosen for this task was Frederick Etchells, an old Bloomsbury friend and a contributor to the Omega Workshop.

However, voices were raised against the project, notably by the Hon Mrs Nancy Sandilands of Five Elms, Berwick, who claimed that there was strong opposition to it among parishioners. Two days before her appeal against the advisory committee's decision was due to be heard Bishop Bell invited everyone concerned to a meeting in the village school to discuss the designs. Vanessa feared that Mrs Sandilands was about to denounce her as an atheist and someone living in sin, but it transpired that the real reason for her opposition was that she thought Quentin was a conscientious objector. When it was made clear that he had been pronounced unfit for military service because of tuberculosis, and was doing approved war work on the land, the opposition collapsed. The consistory court's consent to the scheme was given by Sir Kenneth Clark, Frederick Etchells and the president of the Sussex Archaeological Society — at that time the Rt Rev Hugh Hordern, Bishop of Lewes.

Department store owner Peter Jones gave financial assistance for the murals and John Christie of Glyndebourne supplied large easels for the panels, which were painted on plasterboard in Maynard Keynes's barn at Tilton.

Friends, family and neighbours were pressed into service as models for the artists and for the painting of Bishop Bell a life size model made of chicken wire and papier mache was used.

On the north wall of the nave is *The Nativity*, painted by Vanessa Bell. The Holy Family is pictured inside the Tilton barn with Mount Caburn seen through the open door. A Pyecombe hook, best known of all the Sussex shepherds' crooks, and a Sussex trug, the distinctive wooden basket made at Herstmonceux, give the painting strong links with the locality.

Two shepherds, each with only one arm as the result of action in the 1914–18 war, Charleston housekeeper Grace Higgens, her husband and son, and the two sons of the one armed shepherds were Vanessa's models for *The Nativity* and she borrowed some lambs from a neighbouring farm.

On either side of the chancel arch are paintings by Duncan Grant. On the north side are the kneeling figures of a soldier, a sailor and an airman. The models for these were Douglas Hemming, who was killed in the D-Day invasion in 1944, and two local men named Weller and Humphry. On the south side Bishop Bell is pictured with the then rector of Berwick, the Rev George Mitchell. Over the chancel arch is Duncan Grant's painting of *Christ in Glory*.

The Annunciation, by Vanessa Bell, is on the south wall of the nave. Her daughter posed for the Virgin and Angelica's friend, the actress Chattie Salaman, was the model for the angel. Through the window behind the figures is the walled garden at Charleston.

The Victor of Calvary, by Duncan Grant, is on the west wall. The artist has captured Christ's triumph over death in a crucifixion painted on a chalice-shaped panel. There is no tension in the limbs, Christ's head is erect and his arms are outstretched in the Jewish attitude of prayer. His eyes are open and on his face is a slight smile. The artist Edward Le Bas, who was tied to an easel, was the model.

Duncan Grant's typical Sussex scenes of the four seasons, and of dawn and sunset, are mounted on the chancel screen. Originally the pulpit carried three Vanessa Bell panels, but these were destroyed by vandals in 1962 and Duncan Grant painted replacement panels of fruit and flowers to designs by Angelica Garnett.

Inside the chancel all the paintings are by Quentin Bell. Behind the altar is *Supper at Emmaus*, with a Downland scene in the background. Two men from the Anzac forces stationed with the searchlight battery in Firle Park during the war posed as models for the disciples and a friend of the artist was the model for Christ.

Chattie Salaman was again a model for Quentin Bell's painting *The Wise and Foolish Virgins* on the reverse of the chancel arch. Below, the *Cycle of Life* depicts life from cradle to grave. The altar cloth was designed by Duncan Grant and worked by his mother, Ethel.

When they were completed the panels were mounted directly on to the walls, but after some damage occurred through damp they were removed, framed and replaced. Some time after the panels were installed the artists returned to paint circular tromp l'oeil windows in the nave and coloured bands around the arches and on the chancel screen.

'It's like stepping out of foggy England into Italy,' said Charles Reilly when he saw the murals for the first time.

In the churchyard is the grave of the Rev E Boys Ellman, most notable of the church's rectors. In 1846 he took on a derelict building with broken spire, its bells on the floor, a bricked-up north aisle and a tumble-down east end with a makeshift thatched roof. The only side that let in any light, the south, had earth up to the windows. Ellman completed a remarkable restoration during his incumbency, which lasted until 1906. He also restored the elegant rectory, and built the village school. The rectory was sold in 1963 and a new parsonage was built in its walled vegetable garden.

Visitors to St Michael and All Angels may park in a flower bordered, flint walled car park where the rector's old mounting block can still be seen.

The Nativity by Vanessa Bell

(Jim Redman)

The Annunciation by Vanessa Bell

(Jim Redman)

81

The Victor of Calvary by Duncan Grant
(Jim Redman)

Christ in Glory and the chancel arch paintings by Duncan Grant
(Jim Redman)

Supper at Emmaus by Quentin Bell

(Jim Redman)

WHO'S WHO IN BLOOMSBURY

ANREP Helen, 1885–1965, wife of mosaicist Boris von Anrep, mistress of Roger Fry.

BELL Vanessa, 1879–1961, painter, daughter of Sir Leslie Stephen, sister of Virginia Woolf, married Clive Bell in 1907. Mother of Julian 1908–1937 and Quentin 1910– by Clive Bell and Angelica, 1918– by Duncan Grant.

BELL Arthur Clive Heward, 1881–1964, art critic and author.

BELL Quentin, 1910– , artist, author, professor of English.

BIRRELL Francis, 1889–1935, literary editor of National and Athenaeum.

CARRINGTON Dora, 1893–1932, artist.

ELIOT Thomas Stearns, 1888–1965, American-born poet, editor of The Criterion.

FORSTER Edward Morgan, 1879–1970, novelist.

FRY Marjorie, 1874–1958, one of Roger Fry's six sisters; a JP, prison reformer and literary executor of her brother's work.

FRY Roger Eliot, 1866–1943, painter, art critic, introduced Post-Impressionism to Britain.

GARNETT Angelica, 1918– , daughter of Vanessa Bell and Duncan Grant, actress, painter.

GARNETT David (Bunny), 1892–19, married Ray Marshall (d 1940), married Angelica Bell 1942.

GRANT Duncan James Corrowr, 1885–1978, painter; lived with Vanessa Bell from 1914 until her death; father of Angelica Bell.

HUTCHINSON Mary, 1889–1977, a Strachey cousin, married St John Hutchinson 1910; Clive Bell's long-term mistress.

KEYNES John Maynard, 1883–1946, economist, university lecturer, senior civil servant; married Russian dancer Lydia Lopokova 1925

LOPOKOVA Lydia, 1892–1981, dancer with Diaghilev's Ballet Russes.

MACCARTHY Charles Otto Desmond, 1877–1952, journalist and literary editor of The New Statesman; pen name Affable Hawk; married Mary Warre-Cornish in 1906.

MACCARTHY Mary (Molly), 1992–1953, writer, author.

MORRELL Lady Ottoline, 1873–1938, patron of the arts, married Philip Morrell, mother of one daughter, Julian, born 1906.

NICOLSON Harold 1886–1968, son of first Baron Carnock; diplomat and author, married Victoria Sackville-West 1913, by whom he had two sons.

SACKVILLE-WEST, Victoria Mary (Vita), 1892–1962, only child of third Baron Sackville; novelist, poet, garden designer.

STEPHEN Adrian Leslie, 1883–1948, psychologist; younger brother of Vanessa Bell and Virginia Woolf, married Karin Costello, father of two daughters, Ann and Judith.

STRACHEY, Giles Lytton, 1880–1932, critic and biographer, author of Eminent Victorians, Queen Victoria and Books and Characters.

STRACHEY James Beaumont, 1887–1976, psychoanalyst, Lytton's youngest brother; English translator of Freud.

SIDNEY-TURNER Saxon, 1880–1962, a civil servant.

WOOLF Leonard, 1880–1969, author, journalist, publisher; married Virginia Stephen 1912.

WOOLF Virginia, 1882–1941, author, essayist, publisher.

Friends and acquaintances of the Bloomsbury Group included Amabel and Clough Williams-Ellis (she was a Strachey, he an architect and creator of Portmeirion); Lord Tweedsmuir (novelist John Buchan) and Lady Tweedsmuir; Edith and Osbert Sitwell; Stephen Spender; Kingsley Martin; Enid Bagnold; Bertrand Russell; Vera Britain; George Bernard Shaw; Dame Ethel Smyth; Robert Helpmann; Frederick Ashton; Anthony Blunt; Rupert Brooke; Vivien Leigh; Hugh Walpole.

BIBLIOGRAPHY

Among books consulted are:

Virginia Woolf, a biography, Volume I, Quentin Bell, *(The Hogarth Press, 1972).*

The Flowers of the Forest, David Garnett, (Chatto and Windus, 1955).

With Duncan Grant in Southern Turkey, Paule Roche, (Honeyglen, 1982).

Beginning Again, Leonard Woolf, (The Hogarth Press, 1964).

Downhill all the Way, Leonard Woolf, (The Hogarth Press, 1967).

The Journey not the Arrival Matters, Leonard Woolf, (The Hogarth Press, 1969).

The Flight of the Mind, Volume I of the letters of Virginia Woolf,
    ed. Nigel Nicolson, (The Hogarth Press, 1975); *The Question of Things Happening, Volume II,* (1976); *A Change of Perspective, Volume III,* (1977); *A Reflection of the Other Person, Volume IV,* (1978); *The Sickle Side of the Moon, Volume V,* (1979); *Leave the Letters Till We're Dead, Volume V,* (1980).

The Diary of Virginia Woolf, Volumes I, II, III IV, ed. Anne Olivier Bell,
    (The Hogarth Press, 1976, 1978, 1980, 1982).

A Very Close Conspiracy, Jane Dunn, (Jonathan Cape, 1990).

The Loving Friends, David Gadd, (The Hogarth Press, 1974).

Vanessa Bell, Hilary Spurling, (George Weidenfeld & Nicolson Limited, 1983).

A Boy at The Hogarth Press, Richard Kennedy, (Heinemann, 1972).

A Cezanne in the Hedge, ed. Hugh Lee, (Collins and Brown, 1992).

Duncan Grant and the Bloomsbury Group, Douglas Blair Turnbaugh,
    (Bloomsbury Publishing, 1987).

Virginia Woolf and Lytton Strachey — Letters, ed. Leonard Woolf and James
    Strachey, (The Hogarth Press and Chatto and Windus, 1956).

John Maynard Keynes, Volumes I and II, Robert Skidelsky, (Macmillan 1983 and 1992).

Omega and After, Isabelle Anscombe, (Thames and Hudson, 1981).

Recollections of Virginia Woolf, ed. Joan Russe, (Owen, 1972).

A Postillion Struck by Lightning, Dirk Bogarde, (Chatto and Windus, 1977).

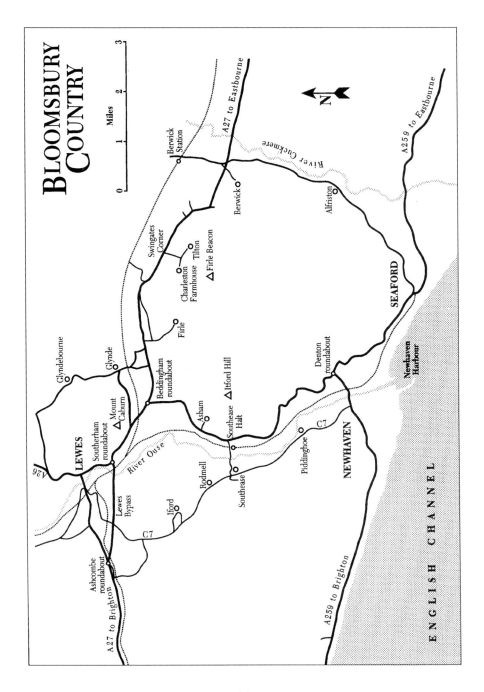

GETTING THERE

THE BLOOMSBURY TRAIL begins in the county town of Lewes, heart of Bloomsbury country. In the town itself are two places to see.

One is the Round House in Pipe Passage — a private residence not open to the public. The passage is off the upper High Street, opposite The Brewers public house. Parallel with Pipe Passage, and just a few feet to the west, is public parking in Westgate.

The other place of interest is the Market Tower, which contains the Julian Bell painting of Tom Paine. Entrance to the tower, which serves as a walk-through, is next to the Crown Hotel, opposite the war memorial in the centre of the High Street.

For Monks House, take the C7 road south from Lewes. Rodmell is four miles distant, and Monks House is the last building on the right, at the far end of the village.

For Charleston Farmhouse, take the A27 east out of Lewes — it will be found signposted on the right, a short distance on from the Firle farm shop.

For Berwick Church, travel a further two miles on from Charleston Farmhouse on the A27, and look for a signpost on the right. The church is at the end of the village and has its own car-park.

For Firle village, again take the A27 from Lewes, and the turn-off is on the right (before Charleston), a mile or so from the Beddingham roundabout. Talland House, a private residence, not open to the public, is on the left, opposite the village hall; and the church is at the end of the village. The graves of Vanessa Bell and Duncan Grant are in the north-east area of the churchyard.

Julian Bell putting the finishing touches to his portrait of Tom Paine, May 1994. The painting, now in the Market Tower, Lewes, shows the revolutionary with his upraised arm above Lewes, with the White Hart Hotel prominent, and the River Ouse, in which Julian's great aunt, Virginia Wolf, drowned herself, snaking down to the sea at Newhaven. Paine points west, beyond the Isle of Wight, to America. Over his right shoulder is Continental Europe with the Seine leading to Paris where the Bastille is burning

(Angus Hoy)